501

Things <u>YOU</u>
Should Have
Learned
About...

PHILOSOPHY

METRO BOOKS
New York

An Imprint of Sterling Publishing
387 Park Avenue South
New York, NY 10016

WRITTEN BY: Alison Rattle and Alex Woolf
DESIGNER: Clare Barber
EDITOR: Catherine Knight
PUBLISHER: James Tavendale

ISBN 978-1-4351-4078-3

501

Things YOU Should Have Learned About...

PHILOSOPHY

METRO BOOKS
New York

CONTENTS

INTRODUCTION

If we're honest, when we hear the word "philosophy," most of us think of Ancient Greeks lying around in togas or dusty college professors with untrimmed beards. This book will show you that philosophy is a vibrant, fascinating and inspiring subject by introducing you to history's greatest philosophical minds, ideas and puzzles in 501 manageable chunks.

Find out how philosophers from thousands of years ago, including Socrates, Aristotle and Plato, continue to influence how we see the world today. Discover how more modern philosophies, such as Marxism, existentialism and pragmatism, have shaped our global societies, religions and governments. Explore the role philosophy has played in the world's most dramatic turning points, from the revolutions of the eighteenth century to women's liberation.

This book will have you thinking about the deepest questions we can ask ourselves. Who are we? Why are we here? What is reality? In these pages, you'll uncover ideas that have challenged the ways in which we think about ourselves, the world, reality, ethics, religion, language and politics, and the problems and paradoxes that philosophers have been debating for centuries.

Philosophy literally means "love of wisdom," so wake up those brain cells and get thinking!

NIETZSCHE

John Dewey

HEGEL

DESCARTES

MARX

BERKELEY

LEIBNIZ

1 THE PRESOCRATICS

THERE IS NO definitive moment marking the beginnings of philosophy. A popular origin story holds that it began with Thales of Miletus, who successfully predicted the occurrence of an eclipse and claimed that magnets have souls, but it is probably more accurate to say that Thales is the personification of a new way of thinking that emerged in Ancient Greece during the sixth century BC. This thinking emphasized the ordered and logical nature of the world and the importance of reason and argument in the endeavour to understand the nature of things in a deep sense.

2 FAST FACT...

ANAXIMANDER is the first philosopher known to have written down his ideas.

The thinkers who pioneered this new mode of thought are known as the Presocratic philosophers (literally, because they came before Socrates). Amongst their number are luminaries such as Anaximander, Heraclitus, Parmenides and Empedocles. To the modern mind, their ideas appear esoteric and often rather quaint – Anaximander, for example, thought that the basic stuff of the universe is limitless, indeterminate, eternal and invisible, though not any kind of element – but they mark the first faltering steps of humanity's long walk into the light of reason. (*See* Many, One or None, p44)

3 FAST FACT...

 **HERACLITUS** (535–437 BC) buried himself in cow dung to try and cure himself of dropsy.

Ancient ruins at Miletus, Greece

4 CONFUCIUS (551 BC–479 BC)

🎓 **AT ABOUT THE** same time as a few remarkable Greeks began taking the first tentative steps towards rationality, the great Chinese sage, Confucius, was busy developing the ideas that would become the system of thought known as Confucianism. According to tradition, Confucius was born in 551 BC near the city of Ch'ü-fu in the Chinese State of Lu. From a poor but noble warrior family, he lived at a time of great political and social upheaval. The ancient feudal system of the Zhou kingdom had broken up, leaving behind a mess of warring feudal states. Confucius's teachings were an attempt to reverse the moral decay that had occurred as a result of the political and social instability.

5 FAST FACT...

📖 **IN 435 BC** Greek philosopher Anaxagoras was cast out of Athens for suggesting that the sun was a big ball of fire.

6 FAST FACT...

📖 **BEFORE** he became a philosopher, Confucius worked as a shepherd, a cowherd, a clerk, a book-keeper and a politician.

It would be hard to overstate the significance of Confucius's ideas; they remain foundational to Chinese social and cultural life. Although Confucius was not a systematic thinker, it is nevertheless possible to identify a number of key themes in his thought. In particular, he emphasized the importance of virtue and the cultivation of humanity. He believed that developing good everyday relationships would translate positively to the community as a whole. (See Confucianism p45)

7 FAST FACT...

📖 *"Choose a job you love, and you will never have to work a day in your life."* – Confucius (551 BC–479 BC)

8 SOCRATES (470 BC–399 BC)

🎓 **ACCORDING TO LEGEND,** the Oracle of Delphi once pronounced Socrates to be the wisest of all men. In response, Socrates tried to prove the Oracle wrong by approaching those men he considered to be the wisest in Athens and asking them about the virtues. Having reduced each one to confusion, he concluded that perhaps he was the wisest man after all, because at least he knew that he didn't know anything.

9 FAST FACT...

📖 **SOCRATES** may have been wise, but he was not attractive. He is described variously as pug-nosed, thick-lipped and rotund.

This story is a perfect illustration of Socrates's philosophical style. He described himself as a gadfly, buzzing around Athens asking awkward questions, with the aim of shaking the Athenian population out of its complacency. The Athenian authorities, however, did not take kindly to his agitation, and eventually he was tried and sentenced to death for the crimes of *"corrupting the youth"* and *"not believing in the city gods."* He met his death in the manner in which he lived, engaging his friends in philosophical discussion, discoursing on the nature of death, and calmly drinking the hemlock that was to kill him. (*See* Socratic Method p46)

Poison hemlock

10 FAST FACT...

📖 *"I know nothing except the fact of my ignorance."* – Socrates (470 BC–399 BC)

RIGHT: Socrates is handed the cup of hemlock that will kill him

11 PLATO (427 BC–347 BC)

🎓 **IF THERE IS** a single philosopher who deserves the title *"the father of philosophy"*, it is Socrates's most famous pupil, Plato. Our knowledge of Plato's life is sketchy, but it seems he was born into a wealthy and well-connected Athenian family in around 427 BC. As far as we can tell, he was destined for a life in public service but turned his back on it, perhaps as a result of the disgust he felt at Socrates's execution, to concentrate on philosophy instead.

This was to our great good fortune as the dialogues he left behind are among classical civilization's greatest achievements. The dialogues are normally organized into three periods. Socrates looms large in the early dialogues and it is believed these reflect Socrates's views and interests rather than Plato's specifically. However, the middle and later dialogues are different, with Plato much more to the fore.

It has been said of the Western philosophical tradition that it is best understood as a series of footnotes to Plato. Certainly it is true that had Plato never lived, the history of philosophy would have been very different. (*See* Theory of Forms, p47)

12 FAST FACT...

📖 **PLATO** was originally called Aristocles, but he was nicknamed Plato (meaning *"broad"*) because of his very wide forehead.

Statue of Socrates,
who was Plato's tutor

13 FAST FACT...

📖 **"COURAGE** is knowing what not to fear." – Plato (427–347 BC)

14 ARISTOTLE (384 BC–322 BC)

BORN IN 384 BC, Aristotle is the most modern of the ancient philosophers. Not only was he the first to argue that rational enquiry should be divided into different domains depending upon the focus of interest, but he also conducted his own groundbreaking work in fields as diverse as ethics, metaphysics, physics, biology, aesthetics, poetry, rhetoric, cosmology and philosophy of mind.

Happily, we know more about Aristotle's life than we do about Plato's. He was a student and teacher at Plato's Academy, then moved to Macedon after Plato's death in 347 BC, where he tutored the future Alexander the Great. He then returned to Athens, where he founded his own school (the Lyceum). Like Socrates, he ran into difficulties with the Athenian authorities, and fled the city declaring that he would not allow the Athenians to *sin twice against philosophy.*

Aristotle is not an easy philosopher. His ideas are complex and his writing is technical, detailed and often obscure. However, his importance is such that no serious student of philosophy can get by without knowing at least something about what he thought. (*See* Four Causes, p48)

15 FAST FACT...

ARISTOTLE studied and contributed to almost every subject possible at the time. His combined works amount to a virtual encyclopedia of Greek knowledge.

16 FAST FACT...

MANY of Aristotle's works might have been lost to us if they hadn't been rediscovered in a dirty pit in 80 BC.

17 AUGUSTINE (354–430 AD)

👨‍🎓 **WE KNOW MORE** about the life of Augustine of Hippo, the father of Christian philosophy, than perhaps we do about any other early philosopher, largely because he told us all about it in his great autobiographical work, *Confessions*. It is here that we learn that Augustine spent much of his youth struggling, not always successfully, with lustful impulses.

18 FAST FACT...

📖 **AUGUSTINE** of Hippo is the patron saint of brewers, printers and the alleviation of sore eyes.

He does not tell us this out of any desire to feed our prurience, but rather because he saw humanity's obsession with sex as being indicative of our sinful nature. Humans are irremediably steeped in sin as a result of Adam's fall. We are not able to rescue ourselves from this state, but must instead depend upon the gift of God's grace. Augustine believed that this would be granted only to an elect few, the rest of humanity being destined to suffer eternal damnation.

These ideas fed into a rather austere world view that came to dominate Christian thinking for over a millennium. Although this had a number of disastrous consequences, there is no doubting Augustine's significance as a thinker. Even today, the idea that it is only by the grace of God that we are able to achieve salvation is a central theme of Christian theology. (*See* The Two Cities, p49)

Adam and Eve and the forbidden fruit

19 FAST FACT...

📖 *"Grant me chastity and continence, but not yet."* – a prayer uttered by Augustine in his youth.

20 AQUINAS (1225–1274)

THOMAS AQUINAS, an Italian Dominican priest and hugely influential philosopher and theologian, was responsible for at least two of the masterworks of Christian philosophy: *Summa contra Gentiles* and *Summa Theologiae*. It is curious, then, that his pathway into a scholarly, religious life included a kidnapping and an encounter with a prostitute.

At the age of 20, Aquinas decided that he wanted to join the Dominican order rather than become the Benedictine abbot of Monte Cassino as his family hoped. The Aquinas family's reaction to this disappointment was to kidnap and imprison him for a year. He was only set free to pursue his own course after he had demonstrated his piety by chasing away a prostitute, who had been hired in a bid to tempt him away from his godly path.

Aquinas died young after he fell off a donkey, but he still managed to write a startlingly large body of work, many millions of words, all told, and is generally considered to be the Catholic Church's greatest theologian. (See Divine Simplicity, p52)

21 FAST FACT...

"Better to illuminate than merely to shine, to deliver contemplated truths than merely to contemplate." – Thomas Aquinas (1225–1274)

22 FAST FACT...

AQUINAS is the patron saint of students and universities.

The ruins of the Aquinas family castle in Italy

23 NICCOLÓ MACHIAVELLI (1469–1527)

🎓† **THE NAME NICCOLÓ MACHIAVELLI** is synonymous with the idea that he puts forward in his signature work, *The Prince*: that it is necessary and justified for a leader to employ brutal cunning in order to secure and retain power. It is less well-known that Machiavelli came to this view as a result of close up and personal experience of the machinations of power in sixteenth-century Italy.

By the age of 29, Machiavelli was already a prominent Florentine diplomat. In 1500, he was sent to the court of Louis XII of France to discuss the problems that Florence had experienced in subduing Pisa, a rebellious city-state. Although Machiavelli did not hold the King of France in high esteem, he was taken aback to discover just how little respect the French had for Florence. His native city was felt to be weak and vacillating, being neither rich enough nor powerful enough to play a major role in foreign affairs.

Machiavelli never forgot this experience and came to the view that serious politics and real power require the strength, courage and capacity to act quickly and decisively. (*See The Prince*, p53)

Niccoló
Machiavelli
(1469–1527)

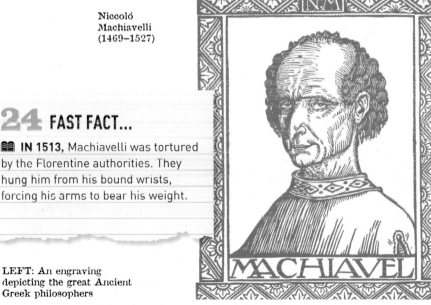

24 FAST FACT…

📖 **IN 1513,** Machiavelli was tortured by the Florentine authorities. They hung him from his bound wrists, forcing his arms to bear his weight.

LEFT: An engraving depicting the great Ancient Greek philosophers

25 RENÉ DESCARTES (1596–1650)

RENÉ DESCARTES, who was born in France at the end of the sixteenth century, is the first great philosopher of modernity. He came to philosophy relatively late in life, and at least partly as a result of his passion for the sciences, but during a 20-year period beginning in 1629, he managed to write a number of the seminal works of modern philosophy.

In the *Discourse on Method*, published in 1637, Descartes laid the foundations of his epistemology and metaphysics. He followed this up in 1641 with the publication of *Meditations on First Philosophy*, in which he articulated his famous "method of doubt" as a mechanism to establish the basis of certain knowledge.

By the time of his death in 1650, his brilliance was well established. His ideas were being taught in universities around Europe; his *Meditations* had included critical contributions from luminaries such as John Locke; and he was well known in the finest intellectual circles of the time. His legacy, though, has surpassed even these promising beginnings. It is fair to say that it is Descartes' work above all others that has shaped the development of philosophy in the modern era. (*See The Cogito*, p54)

26 FAST FACT...

DESCARTES claimed the inspiration for his philosophy came from three powerful dreams he had on the night of November 10–11, 1619.

27 FAST FACT...

"Nothing is more fairly distributed than common sense: no one thinks he needs more of it than he already has."
– René Descartes (1596–1650)

28 BARUCH SPINOZA (1632–1677)

🎓 **IT HAS BEEN** said of the seventeenth-century Dutch philosopher, Baruch Spinoza, that he is the noblest and most loveable of the great philosophers. It is somewhat ironic, then, that for most of his lifetime (and for some considerable time afterwards), Spinoza was considered a man of almost unparalleled wickedness.

29 FAST FACT...

📖 **SPINOZA** lived his life quietly as a grinder of optical lenses, turning down all rewards and honors.

The cause of his troubles was his belief in pantheism – the idea that God is present in everything. This did not go down well in seventeenth-century Europe, indeed until the previous century, pantheism had been considered a formal heresy. Spinoza was publicly excommunicated by Amsterdam's Jewish community, and spent a large part of his life under threat from a religious intolerance that sought to silence him.

Spinoza's magnum opus, *The Ethics*, was published by his friends after his death. It was notable not only for its original philosophy, including a defense of the idea that there is only one substance, an eternal and infinite God, but also for its stylistic mimicry of Euclid's *Elements of Geometry*. (See Divinity and Determinism, p55)

Amsterdam, the Netherlands

30 GOTTFRIED LEIBNIZ (1646–1716)

🎓 **IT IS UNFORTUNATE** for the German philosopher and mathematician Gottfried Leibniz that he is probably best known as the inspiration for Voltaire's satirical creation, Dr. Pangloss, who spends a large part of *Candide* insisting that all is for the best in the best of all possible worlds, despite suffering terrible misadventures. There is an element of truth to this characterization of Leibniz – he was, for example, committed to the view that God could not have made a better world than this one – but it would be wrong to think of him as a fool.

31 FAST FACT...

📖 **AT THE** age of 13, Leibniz composed 300 hexameters of Latin verse in a single morning for a special event at his school.

In fact, his extraordinary ability in a number of different fields is a mark of his intellectual career. Not only did he discover the foundations of differential calculus (independently of Newton), he also invented a calculating machine, designed a variety of pumps that were supposed to drain mines (but which didn't), and carried out important work in physics, geology and even history.

Although he only wrote one book of systematic philosophy (*Theodicy*), many of the concepts and ideas that are now standard in philosophy (for example, the principle of sufficient reason and the identity of indiscernibles), were introduced or anticipated in his work. (*See* The Optimal World, p56)

Gottfried Leibniz (1646–1716)

32 FAST FACT...

📖 **IN 1670**, Leibniz invented the first mechanical calculator that could execute all four basic arithmetical operations.

33 THOMAS HOBBES (1588–1679)

🎓 **THE ENGLISH PHILOSOPHER** Thomas Hobbes, one of history's most influential political philosophers, was fond of relating how he was born prematurely when his mother was frightened into early labor by news of the approaching Spanish Armada. "Fear and I were born twins", he commented, which some people have taken to be a statement about his own normal state of mind. Certainly, fear seems to have played a role in the genesis of his most famous idea; namely, that fear of chaos and death in a state of nature justifies giving up a share of our liberty to a single absolute power (the Leviathan).

34 FAST FACT...

📖 **AFTER GRADUATING** from Oxford, Hobbes went to work for the Cavendish family as a tutor to William Cavendish (1590–1628), who later became the Second Earl of Devonshire.

However, Hobbes was a long way from being a fearful philosopher, as is demonstrated by the number of people he managed to upset during his career. He annoyed Descartes by criticizing his views shortly before the publication of *Meditations*. He upset the Church, and assorted bishops, with his views on free will and the role of the king in interpreting scripture. He also managed to annoy a few atheists by taking the sacrament when he thought he was dying, but actually wasn't. The possibility that he had annoyed even God was seriously entertained for a while, with Parliament wondering whether his work might in some way be responsible for the Great Fire of London. (*See "Nasty, Brutish and Short,"* p58)

Vintage engraving of The Great Fire of London (1666). The fire gutted the medieval city.

35 JOHN LOCKE (1632–1704)

🎓 **JOHN LOCKE**, the father of modern empiricism, is seen by some as the greatest philosopher England has ever produced. Not only did he develop the core concepts of empiricism, in particular, the notion that our minds are blank slates (*tabula rasa*) and that experience alone is the source of all ideas and ultimately of knowledge itself, he also completed important works in political and moral philosophy. Indeed, it is not too much of a stretch to say that without Locke's ideas, the revolutions in America and France, if they had occurred at all, would have looked very different.

Locke lived with the worry that his work might put his life in danger. In 1683, he was forced to flee England after a close associate was tried for treason. It was while he was in exile that he was able to do much of the research that resulted in his great work of political philosophy, *Two Treatises of Government*. It is almost certainly no coincidence that it contained a strong attack on Hobbes' ideas about absolute power. (*See Tabula Rasa*, p59)

36 FAST FACT...

📖 *"Government has no other end but the preservation of property."*
– John Locke

John Locke
(1632-1704)

37 GEORGE BERKELEY (1685–1753)

🎓 **THE CURIOUS THING** about the life of George Berkeley, who famously denied the existence of the material world, is that there is nothing in it to explain how he came to such a radical view. He was born in Kilkenny, Ireland, towards the end of the seventeenth century, attended Trinity College, Dublin, and was ordained into the Anglican Church in 1710. It was at this time that he first made his radical idealism public, setting down his views in *The Principles of Human Knowledge*.

38 FAST FACT...

📖 **THE MOST** popular book Berkeley wrote during his lifetime was his 1744 treatise on the medical benefits of pine tar.

This work was not kindly received. Dr. Samuel Johnson famously made light of his views by kicking a stone and declaring, *"I refute him thus."* Berkeley, however, was not deterred, and published *Three Dialogues between Hylas and Philonous*, in which he carefully went through the rationale for his position. Although he did not win many converts to his view, his arguments were sufficiently ingenious to gain him intellectual respectability, and he was welcomed into London intellectual life.

The idea that reality is at base mental rather than material is highly counterintuitive, of course. However, Berkeley's formulation of this thesis is not the last we'll hear of idealism: the idea returns in even more radical form in the nineteenth century. (See Idealism, p60)

Trinity College, Dublin

39 DAVID HUME (1711–1776)

DAVID HUME has a strong claim to being Britain's greatest philosopher. He is certainly the greatest ever Scottish philosopher; and almost certainly the greatest philosopher of the eighteenth century, which itself was philosophically fertile. He is also the greatest philosopher in the skeptical tradition, and remains a central figure in Western philosophy to this day. It is both ironic and regrettable, then, that he was not particularly widely read in his own lifetime.

40 FAST FACT...

DAVID HOME changed his name to Hume in 1734 because the English found it hard to pronounce "Home" in the Scottish way.

His first book, *A Treatise of Human Nature*, which contains highly novel analyses of free will and personal identity, and a general statement of his sceptical approach, was so spectacularly unsuccessful that Hume himself was driven to lament that *"it fell dead-born from the press."* His follow-up works, *An Enquiry Concerning Human Understanding* and *An Enquiry Concerning the Principles of Morals*, did not fare much better and it was only when he published, *The History of England*, a decidedly non-philosophical affair, that he achieved wide renown.

It is philosophy's loss that Hume did not achieve the recognition he deserved in his own lifetime. If he had been more widely read, it is likely his ideas would have come under close scrutiny, which would have given him reason to write more philosophy. (*See* Skepticism, p61)

Inverness in Scotland, during the 1890s.

41 FAST FACT...

HUME'S great *Treatise of Human Nature* was dismissed by contemporary critics as *"abstract and unintelligible."*

42 JEAN-JACQUES ROUSSEAU (1712–1778)

🎓 **ALTHOUGH JEAN-JACQUES ROUSSEAU** lived as colorful a life as any of the great philosophers, in contrast to his fellow Enlightenment thinkers he was not particularly enamored of the modern world. In fact, he exploded onto the European intellectual scene in 1750, with the publication of an essay titled *Discourse on the Origins and Foundations of Inequality*, in which he argued that the advent of civilization had in various ways undermined the natural goodness of human beings.

This caused a bit of a rumpus in French intellectual circles, since it was seen as a criticism of the Enlightenment idea that the best hope for humanity was the sort of progress that would lead societies to throw off the baggage of a past dominated by superstition and myth. Rousseau did not back away from his criticisms of modernity, but rather fleshed out some of their consequences in his most important work, *The Social Contract*, in which he developed his alternative to the social contract ideas previously articulated by philosophers such as Thomas Hobbes and John Locke. (*See* Noble Savage, p62)

43 FAST FACT...

📖 **AS A TEENAGER,** Rousseau was involved in a *ménage à trois* with noblewoman Françoise-Louise de Warens, 14 years his senior, and the steward of her house.

44 FAST FACT...

📖 *"Fame is but the breath of people, and that often unwholesome."*
– Jean-Jacques Rousseau
(1712–1778)

45 IMMANUEL KANT (1724–1804)

IMMANUEL KANT is perhaps best known for having spent his entire life in Konigsberg (the former capital of Prussia), never traveling more than 50 miles or so from his hometown, and for living a life of such metronomic regularity that it is said the locals of Konigsberg were able to set their clocks by the timing of his afternoon walks.

However, the narrowness of his life stands in dramatic contrast to the scope of his philosophical interests. His magnum opus, *The Critique of Pure Reason*, published in 1881 and generally considered one of the greatest works in the history of philosophy, deals with fundamental questions in epistemology and metaphysics. In addition, he wrote two brilliant works of moral philosophy, and also an important treatment of aesthetics, either of which would have secured his reputation on its own.

The importance of Kant's work was only fully recognized towards the end of his lifetime. However, by the time of his death in 1804, it was becoming apparent that his argument that the mind was actively involved in constituting the empirical world was going to turn out to be every bit the Copernican revolution in philosophy that he had claimed. (*See* Transcendental Idealism, p63)

46 FAST FACT...

📖 *"Act that your principle of action might safely be made a law for the whole world."* – Immanuel Kant (1724–1804)

47 FAST FACT...

📖 **GREATNESS** came to Kant relatively late in life. He published his most important work, *Critique of Pure Reason*, at the age of 57.

48 G. W. F. HEGEL (1770–1831)

BERTRAND RUSSELL has said of the German philosopher, Georg Hegel, that the only reason anybody sane ever accepted his philosophy was because it was so obscure that people thought it must be profound. It is certainly true that *The Phenomenology of Spirit*, probably Hegel's best known work, is almost impossible to understand; and it is also true that Hegel had a huge influence on philosophy in the nineteenth and early twentieth centuries. However, whether or not his ideas are profound is a matter of some controversy.

Part of the difficulty of Hegel's work has to do with what he was trying to achieve with it. Absolute idealism, as his philosophical system came to be known, is a grand theory that aims at explicating not only the relationship between mind and reality, for example, but also the broad sweep of human history. This sort of grandiose system building was popular in the nineteenth century but fell into disrepute in the twentieth, since which time Hegel's stock has fallen quite dramatically. (*See* The Dialectic, p64)

Napoleon Bonaparte

49 FAST FACT...

HEGEL'S brother, Georg Ludwig died while serving as an officer in Napoleon's Russian campaign of 1812.

50 FAST FACT...

"I saw the Emperor – this world soul... who... astride a horse, reaches out over the world and masters it." – Hegel's impression on seeing Napoleon.

51 JOHN STUART MILL (1806–1873)

J. S. MILL is perhaps best known for his advocacy of utilitarianism, which is an ethical theory that holds that an action is right to the extent that it produces the greatest aggregate happiness, and wrong to the extent that it produces the reverse. The difficulty with this formulation is that it lets in the possibility that it might be morally preferable to spend one's time promoting hedonistic pleasures rather than more "civilized" pastimes. Consequently, Mill introduced the notion that certain kinds of pleasure are better than others. Listening to Bach, for example, is a better kind of pleasure than surfing the Internet for pornography; or, as Mill put it, *"it is better to be a human being dissatisfied than a pig satisfied; better to be Socrates dissatisfied than a fool satisfied."*

Moral philosophy was by no means the extent of Mill's intellectual interests. He also did significant work in fields such as jurisprudence, logic, mathematics, language and psychology, and is considered by many to be the foremost English-speaking thinker of the nineteenth century. (*See* Freedom of Speech, p65)

"better to be a human being dissatisfied than a pig satisfied"

52 FAST FACT...

AS PART of his strict upbringing, John Stewart Mill was kept isolated from other children. He could read Greek at the age of 3, and Latin at 8.

53 SOREN KIERKEGAARD (1813–1855)

🎓 **PHILOSOPHY'S "MELANCHOLIC DANE"** (or *"gloomy sod,"* as philosopher Ted Honderich once put it) is not Hamlet, but Soren Kierkegaard, the father of existentialism. A complex and deeply religious thinker, his work was hugely influential on the development of European thought in the twentieth century.

54 FAST FACT...

📖 *"His hair rose almost six inches above his forehead into a tousled crest that gave him a strange, bewildered look."* – a description of the young Kierkegaard

Until Kierkegaard appeared on the scene, philosophy had been in danger of disappearing into a haze of grand, metaphysical speculation. Kierkegaard blew away the clouds by emphasizing the importance of subjectivity, passion, commitment and faith. This emphasis on the subjective dimensions of lived experience can be seen as a precursor of existentialism.

It would be a mistake, though, to think Kierkegaard would have been wholly sympathetic to the views of Sartre and his colleagues. Whereas twentieth-century existentialism tended to be thoroughly atheistic in character, Kierkegaard's work was suffused with religious themes and imagery, most notably encapsulated in his avowal of the moral significance of a *"leap of faith."*

Copenhagen, Denmark

55 FAST FACT...

📖 **THOUGH** he loved her, Kierkegaard broke off his engagement to Regine Olsen in 1841, believing his *"melancholy"* made him unsuitable for marriage.

56 KARL MARX (1818–1883)

🎓 **THERE ARE NOT** many philosophers who can be seen as responsible for the way the history of an entire century unfolded, but this is the position Karl Marx enjoys in relation to the twentieth century. The revolutions that took place in Russia and China were both ostensibly inspired by the writings of Marx, and the Cold War saw Western capitalist countries battling for power against countries that identified themselves as socialist or communist.

Marx wrote with the intention of affecting history. *The Communist Manifesto* contains the following call to arms, for example:

Let the ruling classes tremble at a communist revolution. The proletarians have nothing to lose but their chains. They have a world to win. Workers of all countries, unite!

57 FAST FACT...

📖 **AS A YOUNG** man, Karl Marx served as co-president of the Trier Tavern Club Drinking Society.

This overt political aspect does rather raise the question of whether Marx can properly be considered a philosopher, to which the most plausible response is that he wasn't a pure philosopher, but there is nevertheless plenty of philosophical interest in his work. (*See* Class Struggle, p66)

58 FAST FACT...

📖 *"The philosophers have only interpreted the world...the point however is to change it'"*– Karl Marx in *The Communist Manifesto* (1948)

WORKERS OF ALL LANDS

59 FRIEDRICH NIETZSCHE (1844–1900)

🎓 **IN 1889**, Friedrich Nietzsche, who had written such luminous works as *Thus Spake Zarathustra* and *Beyond Good and Evil*, watched as a coachman whipped his horse in the Piazzo Carlo Aberto in Turin. This was more than Nietzsche could bear: he flung himself around the horse's neck and fell in a heap. Madness had come upon him, and he would never write another sane word.

Nietzsche's insanity was tragic, but not surprising. Life had been a struggle right from the start as his father had lost his mind when the young Friedrich was just five years old. Though Nietzsche excelled at school and university, and managed to secure the Chair in Philosophy at the University of Basel when he was only 24, throughout this time he suffered from chronic, debilitating ill health.

Eventually, this took its toll, and Nietzsche was forced to quit the university in 1879. He spent the next 10 years of his life trudging around the boarding houses of Germany, Italy and Switzerland, frequently alone, and constantly sick. However, this was an extraordinarily fertile time. In his final active year, he was able to complete *The Case of Wagner*, *Twilight of the Idols*, *The Antichrist*, *Ecco Homo* and *Nietzsche Contra Wagner*. (See Ubermensch, p68)

60 FAST FACT...

📖 **SERVING** as a medical orderly during the Franco-Prussian War (1870–1), Nietzsche contracted diphtheria, dysentery and possibly syphilis.

61 FAST FACT...

📖 *"A pair of powerful spectacles has sometimes sufficed to cure a person in love."* – Nietzsche

62 WILLIAM JAMES (1842–1910)

🎓 **WILLIAM JAMES**, an American philosopher and psychologist, spent a large chunk of his early life struggling with his own mental health issues. In part, this appears to have been a consequence of his prodigious abilities in many different fields of endeavor, which meant that it was only in his early middle-age that he finally decided what he wanted to do with his life.

It seems that James was saved from despair because of something akin to a philosophical epiphany. He had been worrying about the consequences of determinism, and in particular the possibility that life is pointless if our every action and thought are merely the effect of prior events, when he came across the work of Charles-Bernard Renouvier, and in it found a novel take on the issue. Renouvier argued that free will involves choosing to focus the mind on some thought, which then motivates an action, in a situation where it is possible to have other thoughts. This led James to the view that neither free will nor determinism can be shown to be true, but there is nevertheless room for a kind of freedom that is related to the practical consequences of adopting one position rather than another. (*See* Pragmatism, p71)

63 FAST FACT...

📖 **WILLIAM JAMES** suffered from problems with his eyes, back, stomach and skin. He was also tone deaf and, at times, suffered from suicidal depression.

64 JOHN DEWEY (1859–1952)

THE PHILOSOPHER Richard Rorty once defined truth as *"whatever one's contemporaries let one get away with."* Although, presumably, he was not being entirely serious, there are philosophers who deny that truth is to be found in the correspondence between truth-claims and states of affair in the world. John Dewey was one such philosopher.

According to Dewey, the measure of any true belief is that it provides successful rules of conduct in our dealings with the world. Most of the time we are able to get by in our daily lives by drawing upon established habits and knowledge. However, occasionally we face situations of genuine doubt, and it is this that motivates further enquiry and the production of new knowledge.

Enquiry proceeds first by means of hypothesis development, which is a creative process since it requires thinking beyond what is given in a problematic situation, and then through the empirical testing of hypotheses. This process concludes with the incorporation of new knowledge into the existing framework of habits, which allows people to act in accordance with the events in their lives. Truth is that which works. (See Progressive Education, p69)

65 FAST FACT...

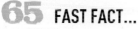

JOHN DEWEY is the only philosopher to have appeared on a US postage stamp.

66 GEORGE SANTAYANA (1863–1952)

🎓 **EVEN IF YOU** know nothing about the Spanish-born philosopher George Santayana, you will probably be familiar with at least one thing he said, since it is in his work, *Reason and Common Sense*, that we find the warning that *"those who cannot remember the past are condemned to repeat it."* It is probably true to say that Santayana is nowadays better known for his aphorisms and literary works than for his philosophy, but nevertheless he remains a significant figure in the tradition of American pragmatism.

67 FAST FACT...

📖 **SANTAYANA** wrote a bestselling novel, *The Last Puritan*, in 1935, and was able to live comfortably off the proceeds for the rest of his life.

68 FAST FACT...

📖 *"There is no cure for birth and death save to enjoy the interval."'*
– George Santayana (1863–1952)

Santayana advocated for a certain kind of honesty in philosophy. He rejected the abstract, metaphysical posturing characteristic of much European thought at the time, campaigning instead for a philosophy that was located in the lived world, right "in the middle of things." The job of the philosopher is not to aim at establishing unquestionable truths, since this would be a futile exercise, but rather to uncover the beliefs that are presupposed by the way we behave in the world. (*See* On Beauty, p70)

Wittgenstein's first great work, Tractatus Logico-Philosophicus, was written while he was serving on the eastern front in World War I.

69 LUDWIG WITTGENSTEIN (1889–1951)

LUDWIG WITTGENSTEIN is considered by many to be the twentieth century's most important philosopher. This makes it a little ironic that what is perhaps best-known about his life is that he once threatened fellow philosopher, Karl Popper, with a poker during an argument over moral rules at the Cambridge Moral Science Club. This event is entirely in keeping with a life that was lived with a compelling, if somewhat disturbing, intensity.

70 FAST FACT...

LUDWIG WITTGENSTEIN (unlike William James) had perfect pitch, and could whistle lengthy and detailed musical passages.

Wittgenstein's first great work, *Tractatus Logico-Philosophicus*, was written while he was serving on the eastern front in World War I. After the book was published in 1922, Wittgenstein gave up philosophy to become a (rather violent) schoolteacher and a gardener. He came back to it after discussions with the Vienna Circle group of philosophers led him to believe that the approach he had taken in the *Tractatus* was thoroughly misguided.

This resulted in the second phase of his career, during which he taught at Cambridge, and pioneered the approach that would become "ordinary language philosophy" after World War II. (*See Language Games, p72*)

71 FAST FACT...

"Eternal life belongs to those who live in the present."
– Ludwig Wittgenstein (1889–1951)

72 MAHATMA GANDHI (1869–1948)

MAHATMA GANDHI was among the most influential of twentieth-century leaders. His philosophy of non-violent protest, and his example in showing how political change might be brought about without violence, inspired a generation of political leaders including Martin Luther King and Albert Lithuli. After his death by assassin's bullet in 1948, Jawaharlal Nehru, a future prime minister of India, famously declared that *"the light has gone out of our lives and there is darkness everywhere."*

Although Gandhi was not a philosopher, his name is inextricably linked with the philosophy of non-violence he championed. This had its roots in Plato, Tolstoy, and particularly, in Hinduism and Jainism. It is easy to lose sight of just how radical Gandhi's non-violent beliefs actually were. This is the advice he gave to *"Every Briton"* in 1940:

"I want you to fight Nazism without arms...You will invite Herr Hitler and Signor Mussolini to take what they want of the countries you call your possessions...If these gentlemen choose to occupy your homes, you will vacate them. If they do not give you free passage out, you will allow yourself, man, woman and child, to be slaughtered, but you will refuse to owe allegiance to them." (See Ahimsa, p73)

73 FAST FACT...

GANDHI'S attempts to establish a law practice in Bombay in the 1890s failed because he was too shy to speak up in court.

74 JEAN-PAUL SARTRE (1905–1980)

JEAN-PAUL SARTRE is the definitive existentialist philosopher. His work, which included novels and plays as well as works of original philosophy, deals with all the classic themes of existentialism, in particular, the claim that humans are always and everywhere radically free.

75 FAST FACT...

 *In pranks "there is more destructive power than in all the works of Lenin." – Jean-Paul Sartre*

Sartre argued that we do not find it easy to live in the knowledge that we have absolute responsibility for the choices we make. He coined the term "bad faith" (*mauvaise foi*) to refer to the strategies we employ to escape our freedom. Normally this means pretending to ourselves that our choices are in various ways compelled, perhaps because they are required by our job, by social convention or by the responsibilities we have to our families.

The reality, though, is that we can never escape our freedom, nor our awareness of it. The structure of consciousness means that it is always at the centre of our experience. The key to living authentically is to make choices in the awareness that they are our choices and ours alone. (*See* Existentialism, p74)

76 FAST FACT...

JEAN-PAUL SARTRE won both the Légion d'Honneur (1945) and the Nobel Prize for Literature (1964), and declined them both.

77 SIMONE DE BEAUVOIR (1908–1986)

🎓 **IT IS PERHAPS** telling that although the French existentialist philosopher Simone de Beauvoir was responsible for *The Second Sex*, arguably the most important feminist text ever written, she is probably best known to most people as the partner of Jean-Paul Sartre. The irony of this situation is compounded when one considers that the central message of *The Second Sex* is that women tend to be seen as "the Other" of men.

There is, of course, no doubting the intellectual and emotional significance of their relationship. Beauvoir herself has said of it that it was the greatest achievement of her life, and that their comradeship *"made a superfluous mockery of any other bond we might have forged for ourselves."* Nevertheless, it remains true that Beauvoir is a first-rate philosopher and feminist theorist in her own right. *The Second Sex*, controversial enough on publication to be added to the Vatican's Index of Forbidden Books, is rightly credited with having sparked feminism's second wave. Indeed, it is not too much of a stretch to say that if *The Second Sex* had not been written, then neither would later pivotal works of feminist theory such as Betty Friedan's *Feminine Mystique* and Kate Millett's *Sexual Politics*. (*See* Second Sex, p76)

78 FAST FACT...

📖 **AGED 21,** Beauvoir came second to Sartre in a highly competitive post-graduate philosophy exam. She was the youngest person ever to pass the exam.

79 JOHN RAWLS (1921–2002)

🎓 **AMERICAN PHILOSOPHER** John Rawls is arguably – and some would say unarguably – the greatest political and moral philosopher of the twentieth century. His major work, *A Theory of Justice*, first published in 1971, is already considered a core text of political philosophy.

80 FAST FACT...

📖 **AS A CHILD,** Rawls contracted diphtheria and pneumonia. He fatally infected two of his younger brothers, Bobby and Tommy.

In this work, Rawls addresses one of the most thorny moral and political issues, namely, how to reconcile the (often) conflicting demands of freedom and equality. He develops a framework to deal with this issue that relies on the notion of *"justice as fairness."* In particular, he argues that it is possible to identify a *liberty principle* and an *equality principle*. The first holds that every person has an equal right to certain basic liberties (for example, the right to possess personal property). The second holds, roughly speaking, that inequality should only be permitted to the extent that it works to the advantage of the least well off.

A Theory of Justice quickly attracted a considerable amount of attention, and criticisms were readily forthcoming. Robert Nozick's famous defense of libertarianism, *Anarchy, State and Utopia*, for example, is in part a response to Rawls. Needless to say, the issues raised by Rawls's work remain very much part of the currency of twenty-first-century political philosophy. (*See Original Position, p77*)

81 FAST FACT...

📖 **AFTER WITNESSING** the aftermath of the Hiroshima bombing, Rawls turned down a promotion to officer and left the army in 1946 as a private.

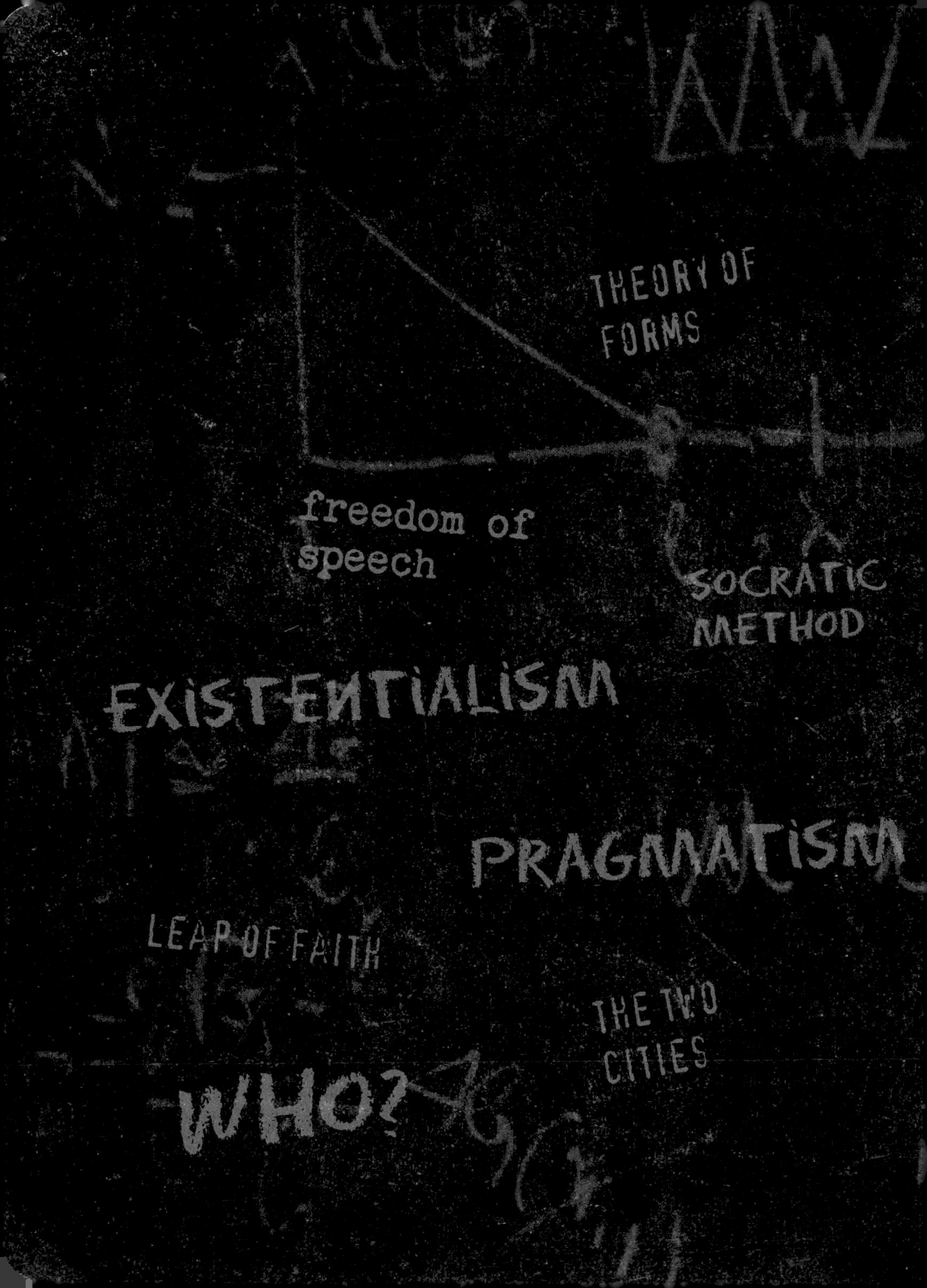

THEORY OF
FORMS

freedom of
speech

SOCRATIC
METHOD

EXISTENTIALISM

PRAGMATISM

LEAP OF FAITH

THE TWO
CITIES

WHO?

82 MANY, ONE OR NONE?

🎓 **PARMENIDES OF ELEA,** perhaps the most important of the Presocratic philosophers, came up with a rather startling idea, namely, that all is One, by which he meant that the universe is singular, indivisible, uniform and unchanging. It might appear as if things move around, come into existence and go out of existence, but according to Parmenides this is an illusion, a consequence of the unreliability of sense experience.

83 FAST FACT...

📖 **AS WELL** as being regarded as the first philosopher in the Greek tradition, Thales was also the first person known to have studied electricity.

This sort of idea was not popular among more sober Greeks, who were fairly certain that there were plural objects in the world and that things did move around. However, the arguments of Parmenides were ingenious and it was difficult to show exactly where he had gone wrong.

Plato indicates that Parmenides's contemporaries came to see him as something of a figure of fun. That may be true, but there is no doubting his philosophical importance. Indeed, Plato's own theory of forms can be seen as an attempt to hold onto the idea that ultimate reality must be unchanging and eternal, while accounting for what sense experience tells us is true about the everyday world of objects. (*See* The Arrow, p228)

84 FAST FACT...

📖 *"It is indifferent to me where I am to begin, for there shall I return again."* – Parmenides

MANY

ONE

NONE!

85 CONFUCIANISM

🎓 **CONFUCIANISM** is a philosophical and ethical system based on the ideas of the Chinese sage, Confucius. It is perhaps best understood as a form of humanism. So, for example, the Confucian ideal of the "perfect gentleman" is the man who exemplifies a properly virtuous life, exhibiting qualities such as fellowship, propriety, righteousness and filial piety.

86 FAST FACT...

📖 **CONFUCIUS** claimed that he never invented anything, merely passed on ancient knowledge. Nevertheless, his idea of meritocracy was revolutionary.

Perhaps the most important concept in the Confucian system is *ren*, which refers to the idea that it is only through loving, faithful and respectful relationships with others that we become fully human. This idea finds its most significant expression in the form of a Golden Rule: do things for others that you would wish them to do for you, and *"what you do not wish for yourself, do not do to others."*

An important point here is that *ren* has a political dimension, since inevitably virtue cultivated in the private sphere will flow into the public realm. It was Confucius' belief that the personal is political in the sense that good behavior cultivated in personal relationships will result in political and social stability. (See Confucius, p11)

87 SOCRATIC METHOD

SOCRATES EMPLOYED a novel method in his attempts to bring wisdom to the Ancient Greeks. He buzzed around Athens demonstrating that although the Athenians thought they knew things, they in fact did not.

His preferred method was to strike up a conversation with a small group of notable citizens about the nature of a concept such as justice or courage. Affecting to be eager to learn something new, he would ask a question. His interlocutor would attempt an answer, but very quickly things would begin to unravel. Socrates would demonstrate that the answer didn't work, or that it was inconsistent with something else the interlocutor believed, or that it was lacking in some other way. This process would tend to continue until everybody was thoroughly confused.

The Greek word for this pattern of engagement is *elenchus*, and Socrates was its ultimate exponent. According to Xenophon, he *"could do what he liked with any disputant."* His motivations, though, are not entirely clear. Presumably, part of his intention was to show that there is merit in knowing that you don't know anything! (*See* Socrates, p12)

88 FAST FACT...

THE ANCIENT GREEK dramatist Aristophanes wrote a play, *The Clouds*, poking fun at Socrates as a man with his head in the clouds.

89 FAST FACT...

THE SOCRATIC METHOD was never intended to solve a problem, only to demonstrate one's ignorance.

90 THEORY OF FORMS

CONSIDER THE QUESTION of what it is that makes a shirt a shirt. It's a garment worn on the upper part of the body, obviously, but suppose the shirt loses both its sleeves, is it still a shirt? Maybe so, but what if the material of which it's made begins to unravel, is there a point at which what remains a no longer shirt? Or what about if it shrinks in the wash to the size of a postage stamp, is it still a shirt then?

It was these sorts of questions that led Plato to develop his Theory of Forms. This posits the existence of a mind-independent realm of ideal entities, of which the things in the world are merely imperfect copies. Thus, there exists a perfect form of shirt, the color red, earthworm, and every other extant entity. Crucially, abstract concepts such as *justice* and *beauty* also have perfect forms, and things in the world are *just* and *beautiful* to the extent that they instantiate their equivalent forms. (*See* Plato, p14)

91 FAST FACT...

📖 *"The unexamined life is not worth living."*
Plato (427–437 BC)

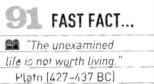

92 FOUR CAUSES

ARISTOTLE STATED that *"we do not have knowledge of a thing until we have grasped its why, that is to say, its cause."* Aristotle was really talking about the explanatory features of an object, the types of thing that can be referred to in answering a *"why"* question.

93 FAST FACT...

📖 **AS WELL** as Alexander the Great, Aristotle tutored Ptolemy and Cassander, who also went on to become crowned kings.

The *material cause* of an object is that out of which it is made (e.g. the bronze of a statue). The *formal cause* refers to the sort of thing an object is – its form (e.g. the shape of a statue). The *efficient cause* of an object is whatever brought it into being or caused it to change (e.g. the sculptor). The *final cause* is the end goal, the *"what it's for"* of the object (e.g. to be displayed as an ornament).

This explanatory framework had a profound effect on the way our understanding of the world developed in the centuries after Aristotle. In particular, the idea that an explanation of a natural phenomenon had to refer to its purpose or goal proved to be a barrier to the emergence of a properly scientific mode of thinking.

94 FAST FACT...

📖 *"Man, when perfected, is the best of animals, but when separated from law and justice, he is the worst of all."* – Aristotle (384–322 BC)

95 THE TWO CITIES

AUGUSTINE OF HIPPO believed that humanity was split into two opposed camps. On the one hand, there is the City of God, which is governed by a love of God, and in virtue of his grace is destined to reign eternally; on the other hand, there is the City of Babylon, which is governed by lust and love of self, and is destined to join the Devil in hell.

Broadly speaking, this division maps onto the division between the Christian Church and the pagan state. There is some complication here, since Augustine is fully aware that mere membership of the Church does not guarantee spiritual and moral virtue. Nevertheless, there is no doubt that Augustine considered the Church to be superior to the state, believing that a state could only be properly just if it manifested Christian principles of conduct. In this sense, Augustine stands against the separation of Church and state, a view which became orthodox in the Middle Ages. (*See* Augustine, p10)

96 FAST FACT...

AUGUSTINE wrote *The City of God* to console Christians after the shocking sack of Rome by the Visigoths in 410 AD.

97 FAST FACT...

"Justice being taken away, then what are kingdoms but great robberies?" – Augustine of Hippo (354–430 AD)

An illustration of Dante's Inferno showing Hell, Purgatory and the City of God.

98 DIVINE SIMPLICITY

🎓 **ACCORDING TO CLASSICAL** theologians such as Thomas Aquinas, God is unlike any extant creature in being without parts. Or, to put it another way, God is divinely simple. The doctrine of divine simplicity is a complex and somewhat bizarre notion, but it can be understood as amounting to the claim that there is no distinction between God and his attributes. God is good, for example, not because he exemplifies the characteristics of goodness, but because he is goodness. Similarly, God is not just because he demonstrates the attributes of justice, but by being justice. Moreover, not only is God identical to each of his attributes, they in turn are identical to each other.

There are a number of advantages to this way of seeing God. In particular, it avoids making God's nature dependent on something external to itself. However, it does come at a cost. The Christian philosopher, Alvin Plantinga, for example, has said of the doctrine that it is *"a dark saying indeed,"* and argues that it depersonalizes God. (*See* Aquinas, p17)

99 FAST FACT...

📖 **WHEN A PROSTITUTE** was sent to Thomas Aquinas's room to test his purity, he chased her away with a burning stick.

100 THE PRINCE

🎓 **THE PRINCE,** a study in the art of leadership, is Niccoló Machiavelli's signature work. First published in 1532, its core thesis is that successful rulers cannot afford to be restricted by the desire to act virtuously all of the time. Rather, the political leader *"must not mind incurring the scandal of those vices without which it would be difficult to save the state."* Hence Machiavelli admired the way in which Cesare Borges employed deception in order to trap and murder leaders of the Orsini faction, who had been plotting against him.

101 FAST FACT...

📖 *"Old Nick"* became an English term for the devil, thanks to the notorious reputation of Niccoló Machiavelli's *The Prince*.

Machiavelli's basic view seems to have been that politics is a dirty business – people do not behave well. If you attempt to lead virtuously, you are almost certainly going to come unstuck and potentially do more damage than you would have done had you simply set out to maintain and secure your own power.

However, Machiavelli did not think that absolutely everything was justified. The best leaders use their power for good reasons, not just because they have the power to act. (See Niccoló Machiavelli, p19)

King Henry VIII (1491–1547) trampling on the figure of Pope Clement VII (1478 - 1534) who refused to grant Henry a divorce from his first wife.

102 FAST FACT...

📖 **HENRY VIII** of England was influenced by *The Prince* in his method of dealing with the Pilgrimage of Grace, a popular uprising in 1536.

103 THE COGITO

IN MEDITATIONS *on First Philosophy*, René Descartes sought to identify at least one belief that it would be impossible to doubt. His technique was to examine each one of his beliefs in turn, abandoning those he could imagine not being true. So, for example, he was able to discount all his sensory experiences, on the grounds that he could be dreaming yet not know it. More radically, he argued that it is possible we're being deceived by an evil demon and literally everything we take to be real is actually an illusion.

The good news is that by means of this technique, Descartes did claim to have identified the one thing it is not possible to doubt, namely, that he existed. In the very act of doubting, we demonstrate that there must be an *"I"* that is doing the doubting. This resulted in his famous *cogito ergo sum* (I am thinking, therefore, I exist), which is the immovable point that constitutes the foundation of all knowledge. (*See* René Descartes, p20)

August Rodin's statue, The Thinker (1902)

104 FAST FACT...

DESCARTES' idea that we might all be being deceived by a malignant being has influenced modern films such as *The Matrix* and *Twelve Monkeys*.

105 FAST FACT...

DESCARTES' success as a mathematician inspired him to believe he could use the same methods to deduce truth in all other disciplines.

106 DIVINITY AND DETERMINISM

🎓 **ACCORDING TO BARUCH SPINOZA,** human beings are aspects of an infinite God. This idea has radical implications for how we view some of the standard themes of Christian theology, and particularly for ideas surrounding concepts such as free will, sin and death.

Spinoza had no time for common sense notions of free will, arguing that people who think that *"they speak or keep silence or act in any way from the free decision of their mind, do but dream with their eyes open."* It is only because we do not know the real causes of our actions that we are able to hold onto this dream.

This does not mean, however, that our existence is pointless. According to Spinoza, we should aim to see reality as God sees it, from the perspective of eternity. If we do this, then our everyday concerns will fade into the background and we will gain a kind of freedom in recognizing our place in the larger whole. (*See* Baruch Spinoza, p21)

107 THE OPTIMAL WORLD

🎓 **GOTTFRIED LEIBNIZ** argued that God's perfection meant that he could not have created a better world than the one that actually exists. On the face of it, this claim seems a little implausible since it is easy to imagine that the world would be a better place without natural disasters, famine or war. The existence of evil in the world seems to rule out both the idea that this is the best of all possible worlds and the existence of an omni-benevolent and all-powerful God.

108 FAST FACT...

📖 **LEIBNIZ** designed several ingenious wind- and water-powered pumps for draining mines. Unfortunately, none of them worked.

Leibniz was aware of this problem and developed a number of responses to it. For example, he argued that we are simply not in a position to know what the consequences would be of eradicating any particular evil from the world. He also denied that human happiness was necessarily the right thing to focus on in determining the goodness of the world. Instead, he suggested that the best world might be the one that is the *"simplest in hypotheses and the richest in phenomena."* (See p22)

Leibniz's theory that this is the best of all possible worlds is difficult to accept given the existence of devasting natural disasters such as volcanoes, floods and drought.

109 NASTY, BRUTISH AND SHORT

🎓 THOMAS HOBBES seemingly held a profoundly jaundiced view of human nature. He argued that in a state of nature, with no curbs on our freedom, we would end up tearing each other apart: there is *"no knowledge of the face of the earth; no account of time; no arts; no letters; no society; and which is worst of all, continual fear, and danger of violent death; and the life of man, solitary, poor, nasty, brutish, and short."*

The only rational response to this situation is to exchange a proportion of our freedom for peace and security. Hobbes claimed that this could be achieved by signing up to a *"social contract,"* which in effect transfers the absolute freedom of the people to a single entity (the great Leviathan), which then uses its power to ensure peace and security for everybody.

Hobbes argued that sovereign power has to be absolute, since it is only absolute power that affords proper protection against the barbarity of a state of nature. (*See* Thomas Hobbes, p23)

110 FAST FACT...

📖 **FOLLOWING** the Great Plague and the Great Fire of London, many people seriously wondered whether Hobbes's writings had provoked God's wrath.

111 FAST FACT...

📖 *"In the first place, I put for a general inclination of all mankind a perpetual and restless desire of power ... that ceaseth only in death."*
– Thomas Hobbes (1588–1679)

The biblical brothers Cain and Abel fighting

112 TABULA RASA

🎓 **IN CONTRAST** to philosophers such as Plato and Descartes, John Locke claimed that all knowledge is ultimately derived from experience. At birth, our mind is a *"blank slate"* (*tabula rasa*), which is then furnished by sensory experience and reflection on simple ideas, out of which more complex ideas and knowledge are formed.

113 FAST FACT...

📖 **LOCKE** was so secretive and suspicious of others that he often wrote in code using invisible ink. Many of his papers were published anonymously.

According to Locke, ideas are either simple or complex. A simple idea is *"nothing but one uniform appearance or conception in the mind,"* perhaps the red of a tomato or sweetness of a peach, for example. Complex ideas are composed of multiple simple ideas. Imagine, for example, the entire experience of eating an apple (its taste, touch, smell, color). The mind is incapable of generating simple ideas on its own, but it can produce complex ones by combining and shifting its bank of simple ideas and remembered experiences.

A key point here is that we have direct knowledge of *ideas*, not of the objects to which these ideas apparently refer. (*See* John Locke, p24)

114 FAST FACT...

📖 **LOCKE** fled England for Holland in 1683 after his friend and patron, the Earl of Shaftesbury, was tried for treason.

115 IDEALISM

IF LOCKE was right, and we only have direct knowledge of ideas rather than objects, it leads to a problem. How do we know that anything exists beyond our ideas? Maybe the world is mental rather than material.

This is the position taken by George Berkeley, who simply denied that the material world had any existence outside of our minds. He argued that what we take to be the objects of the material world exist simply because they are perceived – *"to be is to be perceived."* He uses a variety of arguments to substantiate this claim. For example, he suggests that since our perception of heat is partly determined by whether we ourselves (or parts of our body) are hot or cold, it follows that *"heat and cold are only sensations existing in our minds."*

Perhaps the greatest difficulty for Berkeley's account is to explain how objects persist when they are not being perceived. His answer is that all our ideas are an effect of the will of God. God is all-seeing, and therefore is able to bring the world of ideas into existence. (*See* George Berkeley, p25)

116 FAST FACT...

"That there is no such thing as what philosophers call material substance, I am seriously persuaded." – George Berkeley (1685–1753)

117 SKEPTICISM

DAVID HUME is almost certainly the greatest philosopher in the skeptical tradition. His skepticism saw him deploying arguments against the possibility of inductive knowledge, miracles and God. He also suggested that the common way of thinking about the self and personal identity is mistaken.

The problem of personal identity is as follows. We tend to think that the self endures across time; to put it simply, we are inclined to believe that in some deep sense we are the same person now as we were 10 years ago, and that we will still be this same person into the future. Hume recognizes that we have this idea of personal identity, but can't find anything to justify our confidence in it. If we introspect and focus upon the contents of conscious experience, all we find is an ever-changing bundle of perceptions, but no enduring self. Hume therefore concludes that our common sense notion of the self is a convenient fiction, but no more than that. (See David Hume, p26)

118 FAST FACT...

THE UNIVERSITY of Edinburgh blocked Hume's professorship on charges of atheism and immorality. He never held an academic post.

119 FAST FACT...

"Generally speaking, the errors in religion are dangerous; those in philosophy only ridiculous." – David Hume (1711–1776)

120 THE NOBLE SAVAGE

JEAN-JACQUES ROUSSEAU departed radically from the Hobbesian view that people are innately self-interested and aggressive and that a state of nature would be characterized by *"nasty, brutish and short"* lives (*see* p58).

Instead, he argued that human beings were originally *"noble savages,"* peaceful, solitary and taken up with the demands of day-to-day living. The problems that modern humans experience are in fact a function of social existence and the inequality that comes along with it.

In particular, it was the emergence of private property that marked the beginning of the end of the noble savage. As soon as somebody claimed ownership of a piece of land, things were bound to go wrong. Civil society would necessarily follow because of the need to justify and regulate private property and the inequality that followed in its wake.

121 FAST FACT...

ROUSSEAU got into trouble in 1762 with the publication of his radical work on education, *Emile*, and was forced to flee Paris.

Moreover, once inequality became entrenched, then competitiveness, jealousy and aggression were bound to appear. (*See* Jean-Jacques Rousseau, p27)

122 FAST FACT...

"...the difference is, that the savage lives within himself while social man lives outside himself and can only live in the opinion of others..." – Jean-Jacques Rousseau (1712–1778)

123 TRANSCENDENTAL IDEALISM

🎓 **PRIOR TO IMMANUEL KANT'S** arrival on the scene, the orthodox view of the relationship between mind and experience held that it worked in just one direction: the mind simply records what is going on in the world. Kant turned this conception around entirely, arguing instead that the mind actively constitutes the world of experience. The mind shapes and organizes sensory input, turning it into the world of objects situated in space and time, and further molding it in terms of categories such as substance and causality. Put simply, the mind creates the familiar, everyday world that we inhabit. Far from it being the case that the mind conforms to the world, the world in fact conforms to the mind.

Kant argues that our sensory experience is ordered into relations of space and time by the activity of the mind. So space and time are not something out there in the world, but rather they are a part of the structuring apparatus of perception. (*See* Immanuel Kant, p28)

124 FAST FACT...

📖 **KANT'S** dinner parties were strictly timetabled, with sections set aside for political discussion, telling of amusing anecdotes and music.

125 FAST FACT...

📖 *"The senses do not err – not because they always judge rightly, but because they do not judge at all."*
– Immanuel Kant (1724–1804)

Rousseau's notion of the "noble savage" sparked the contemporary imagination. This engraving shows a scene from Chateaubriand's novella, Atala (1801), which denounces Rousseau's concept.

126 THE DIALECTIC

🎓 **G. W. F. HEGEL** argued that we progress towards understanding the nature of the whole of reality – or "Absolute Spirit," as he called it – via a dialectical process, which sees less successful conceptions of reality being incorporated within the improved conceptions that come to replace them.

127 FAST FACT...

📖 **HEGEL'S** systematic approach to life began early. As a schoolboy he kept a diary charting the progress of his reading.

This dialectic is made up of three parts: any given concept or phenomenon (*thesis*) will contain tensions or contradictory aspects (*antithesis*), which necessitate a movement towards resolution (*synthesis*).

A specific thesis (Concept 1) will be inadequate as a description of reality and will contain contradictions that suggest its opposite or antithesis (Concept 2). This tension can only be resolved by means of a movement towards a new synthesis (Concept 3), which maintains the original thesis and antithesis, while negating the original contradiction. According to Hegel, this is a continual process. Concept 3 will become a new thesis, which in turn is flawed as a description of reality, containing within itself its own antithesis, thus a requiring a movement towards a further synthesis. (*See* G.W.F. Hegel, p29)

128 FREEDOM OF SPEECH

🎓 **J. S. MILL** is responsible for what is arguably history's most important liberal defense of the right to free speech. In the second chapter of *On Liberty*, he argues that *"there ought to exist the fullest liberty of profession and discussion, as a matter of ethical conviction, any doctrine, however immoral it may be considered."* He went on to claim that this is the case even in a situation where the whole of humanity is united in thinking that some particular doctrine is morally repugnant. The immorality of an opinion is never in and of itself reason to suppress its expression.

However, Mill did allow that restrictions could be imposed on free speech in those cases where the possibility of harm loomed large. The "harm principle," as it is known, holds that *"the only purpose for which power can be rightfully exercised over any member of a civilized community, against his will, is to prevent harm to others."*

Obviously, this raises the question as to what exactly constitutes harm. It is clear that Mill meant this to be defined very narrowly, referring only to direct harm caused to other people. (*See* John Stuart Mill, p30)

129 FAST FACT...

📖 **MILL CAMPAIGNED** strongly for women's rights and equal access to education for women,

130 FAST FACT...

📖 **MILL SUFFERED** a nervous breakdown at the age of 20. He was cured by reading the story of a boy who became an inspiration to his family after the death of his father.

Lend me your ears!

131 CLASS STRUGGLE

🎓 **ACCORDING TO KARL MARX,** the history of all hitherto existing societies is the history of class struggle. The precise form this struggle takes depends upon the way that production is organized in any given society. Capitalist society is characterized by the existence of two ineluctably opposed classes: the *bourgeoisie*, the owners of the means of production, and the *proletariat*, who own only their own labor power, which they are forced to sell to the bourgeoisie in circumstances they do not choose.

It was Marx's view that capitalism is inherently unstable. It is inevitable that the proletariat will one day wake up to its exploitation, and once it does it has the power to bring about the downfall of society. Specifically, it is the destiny of the proletariat, acting as a class-for-itself, to abolish all class distinctions, ushering in a new form of society – communism – that is based upon the collective ownership of the means of production. Communism represents the end point of class struggle, since it is a society where the great mass of humanity controls the labor process for itself. (*See* Karl Marx, p32)

132 FAST FACT...

📖 **KARL MARX'S** sisters later told how he used to bully them mercilessly, but made up for it by reading them stories.

133 FAST FACT...

📖 *"What the bourgeoisie therefore produces, above all, are its own grave-diggers. Its fall and the victory of the proletariat are equally inevitable."*
– Karl Marx (1818–1883)

134 LEAP OF FAITH

SOREN KIERKEGAARD wasn't particularly impressed with the average Christian believer of his day. They tended to have been born into the religion, paid lip service to its beliefs and maybe turned up at church once a week, but that was about it. This wasn't enough for Kierkegaard. He celebrated the *"knight of faith"*, who was willing to make a profound leap into the realm of faith despite the contradictions and ambiguities that such an act entailed.

Kierkegaard's knight of faith idea is exemplified in the biblical story of Abraham and Isaac. God commands Abraham to kill his son, Isaac. However, doing so means behaving in a way that is entirely outside the normal domain of morals – it requires *"a suspension of the ethical."* Abraham, alone before God, must make a choice: either he remains attached to the ethical sphere or he makes a leap of faith, putting his trust in a higher authority. Having made the leap, the knight of faith knows that the rules of the ethical sphere are not binding. He owes his loyalty to a higher power. (*See* Soren Kierkegaard, p31)

135 FAST FACT...

KIERKEGAARD'S father was a gloomy, pessimistic, deeply religious man. Kierkegaard later described his upbringing as "insane."

The biblical tale of Abraham and Isaac.

136 THE UBERMENSCH

FRIEDRICH NIETZSCHE argued that modernity was threatened by a crisis of values brought about by the death of God. Until God's demise, Christianity had functioned as a buttress against the threat of nihilism, but with the passing of God, the world has become meaningless. We have come to recognize that the divine will, Plato's forms, Enlightenment values, the Kantian imperative, and so on, are nothing but human constructions now broken asunder.

137 FAST FACT...

SO IMPRESSIVE was Nietzsche's intellect that he was offered the Chair in Philology at the University of Basel aged just 24, before he'd even completed his doctorate.

How do we live now that we have given up our belief in absolutes? Nietzsche's answer is embodied in the figure of the Übermensch – the Superman:

"The noble type of man experiences itself as determining values...it knows itself to be that which first accords honour to things; it is value-creating."

The Übermensch is the measure of all things, a creator of new values in the vacuum of nihilism. It is able to cast off the values of the masses, thereby embracing its freedom to create new and better forms of being. (*See* Friedrich Nietzsche, p33)

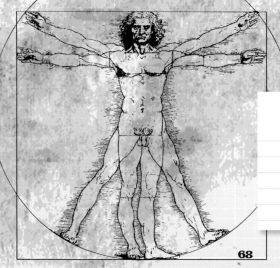

138 FAST FACT...

"'Dead are all gods: now we want the overman to live' — on that great noon, let this be our last will."
– Friedrich Nietzsche (1844–1900)

139 PROGRESSIVE EDUCATION

JOHN DEWEY'S advocacy of progressive and liberal education remains influential to this day. It was his view that education should not aim to inculcate specific skills in a mechanistic fashion, but rather to allow people to develop their full potential and flourish as human beings. Thus, he claimed that to prepare a person for their future means *"to give him command of himself; it means so to train him that he will have the full and ready use of all his capacities."*

There are clear implications here for the specific form education should take. Dewey did not believe that education should be formulaic or overly didactic, since pupils will not flourish if they are treated as passive receptacles to be filled with information. Proper education should aim at cultivating creative thinking and imaginative responses to new situations and information. This will allow people to develop the skills and habits necessary to enable them to function as fully engaged members of democratic societies. (*See* John Dewey, p35)

140 FAST FACT...

"The human being acquires a habit of learning. He learns to learn."
– John Dewey (1859–1952)

141 FAST FACT...

DEWEY was chair of the Commission of Enquiry into charges against Leon Trotsky in the 1930s Moscow trials. The Commission found in favor of Trotsky and against Stalin.

142 ON BEAUTY

🎓 **IN HIS FIRST** major work, *The Sense of Beauty*, George Santayana set himself the task of discovering *"why, when, and how beauty appears, what conditions an object must fulfil to be beautiful, what elements of our nature make us sensible of beauty, and what the relation is between the constitution of the object and the excitement of our susceptibility."*

The theory he developed holds that beauty is the pleasure we get from contemplating an object, where that pleasure is conceived as being an intrinsic part of the object itself. In that sense, beauty is not an empirical fact to be discovered in the world, but rather *"an emotion, an affection of our volitional and appreciative nature.'*

Beauty thus conceived is *"an emotional element, a pleasure of ours, which nevertheless we regard as a quality of things.'"*(See George Santayana, p36)

143 FAST FACT...

📖 *"Beauty as we feel it is something indescribable: what it is or what it means can never be said."*
– George Santayana (1863–1952)

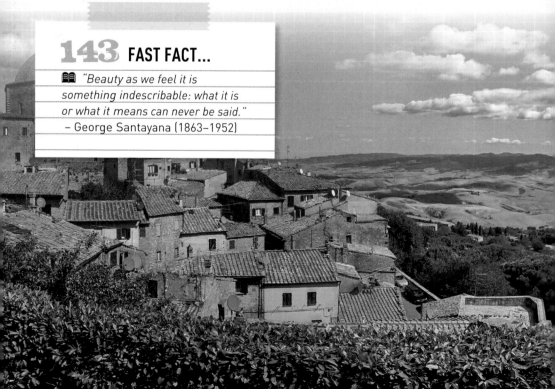

144 PRAGMATISM

IT IS A STRANGE but true fact that a story involving a squirrel is part of the intellectual history of the philosophical position known as pragmatism.

145 FAST FACT...

📖 **WILLIAM JAMES** was able to see almost every side of every argument, leading to near paralysis when it came to making decisions.

William James recounts how he returned from a stroll in the woods to find his friends engaged in a ferocious metaphysical debate about a squirrel. The squirrel is being chased around a tree by a man who is trying to get a glimpse of it. The trouble is every time the man moves, so does the squirrel, so he never sees it. The question his friends are arguing about is whether or not the man goes around the squirrel.

James's response is to ask whether it makes any practical difference. If it does not and the alternatives have the same practical consequences, then there is nothing at stake in the dispute. This is the essence of pragmatism. A belief is true if it works, if it is useful, if it allows us to get on with the business of living. (See William James, p34)

146 FAST FACT...

📖 **JAMES'S** staggering indecisiveness led him to take up teaching, painting, scientific research, medicine and psychology, before settling on philosophy.

147 LANGUAGE GAMES

🎓 **IN HIS FIRST** great work, the *Tractatus*, Wittgenstein developed a *"picture theory of meaning,"* which held that simple propositions (e.g. the dog is on the rug) pick out states of affairs of the world. By the time he came to the end of his career, he was convinced that this theory was fundamentally mistaken.

Rather than conceiving of language as a determinate system that can be specified in precise terms, he came to view it as complex, multifaceted and context-dependent. He argued that the meaning of words is derived at least in part from the context in which they are used. Thus, for example, there is no way of knowing what somebody means when they say *"I hate you!"* unless you know about the context in which it is said.

The notion of language-games is linked to this idea. Wittgenstein argued that different language-games are governed by different rules. He mentioned as examples of language-games: giving and receiving orders, joke telling and cursing. (*See* Ludwig Wittgenstein, p37)

148 FAST FACT...

📖 **WITTGENSTEIN** worked on the manuscript of his first great work, *Tractatus Logico-Philosophicus*, while fighting for Austria on the Eastern Front in World War I.

Where am I?

149 FAST FACT...

📖 **WITH TRACTATUS**, Wittgenstein believed he'd solved all the problems of philosophy, and he gave it up for nine years to be a schoolteacher and a gardener. He later returned to philosophy and wrote his second great work, *Philosophical Investigations*, published posthumously.

150 AHIMSA

AHIMSA is a word derived from Sanskrit literally meaning *"do no harm."* It is an important concept in all Indian religions, and found its most significant modern expression in Mahatma Gandhi's philosophy of non-violence.

Gandhi believed that violence is almost always unnecessary. Human beings are ensouled creatures, so the possibility always exists that their behavior might be changed without resorting to violence. In particular, it was Gandhi's view that it is possible to appeal to the essential humanity of an aggressor by showing them one's own vulnerability and suffering:

151 FAST FACT...

"So long as a man does not of his own free will put himself last among his fellow creatures, there is no salvation for him. Ahimsa is the farthest limit of humility." – Mohandas Gandhi (1869–1948)

...if you want something really important to be done you must not merely satisfy the reason, you must move the heart also. The appeal of reason is more to the head but the penetration of the heart comes from suffering. It opens up the inner understanding in man. Suffering is the badge of the human race, not the sword.

This idea underpinned Gandhi's commitment to non-violent political protest, although, of course, many people will suspect its usefulness is limited to very particular circumstances. (See Mahatma Gandhi, p38)

152 FAST FACT...

GANDHI'S promotion of Ahimsa influenced leaders of civil and political rights movements in other countries, such as Martin Luther King in the USA.

153 EXISTENTIALISM

🎓 **IN HIS** famous lecture, *Existentialism is a Humanism*, Jean-Paul Sartre tells the story of a dilemma faced by one of his students, who was torn between joining the Free French Forces or staying at home to look after his widowed mother. The student was aware his mother would be devastated if he left for the war and also that it was entirely possible his presence amongst the French Free Forces would make no difference to anything. Consequently, he found himself *"confronted by two very different modes of action; the one concrete, immediate, but directed towards only one individual; the other an action addressed to an end infinitely greater, a national collectivity..."*

Sartre argued that there was nothing that could help the student choose which course of action to pursue. He simply had to choose, and thereby invent himself through his choice. This story flags up what is perhaps the key theme of existentialism, namely, that we are absolutely and radically responsible for all our actions. As Sartre put it, we are alone in the world, without excuse. (*See* Jean-Paul Sartre, p39)

154 FAST FACT...

📖 **AS A CHILD**, Sartre had few friends and he spent most of his childhood reading and writing in his grandfather's library.

SELECTED WORKS OF JEAN-PAUL SARTRE

Jean-Paul Sartre was a prolific writer and published numerous plays, novels and critical essays. Sartre declined both the Légion d'honneur (1945) and the Nobel Prize for Literature (1964). He was the first Nobel Laureate to refuse the prize.

1936	The Transcendence of the Ego (*La Transcendance de l'ego*)
1938	Nausea (*La Nausée*)
1939	The Wall (*Le Mur*)
1940	The Imaginary (*L'Imaginaire*)
1943	The Flies (*Les Mouches*)
1943	Being and Nothingness (*L'Être et le Néant*)
1944	No Exit (*Huis-clos*)
1945	The Age of Reason (*L'âge de raison*)
1945–1949	The Roads to Freedom (*Les chemins de la liberté*)
1946	The Respectful Prostitute (*La Putain respetueuse*)
1946	Existentialism is a Humanism (*L'existentialisme est un humanisme*)
1946	Anti-Semite and Jew (*Réflexions sur la question juive*)
1948	Dirty Hands (*Les Mains sales*)
1951	The Devil and the Good Lord (*Le Diable et le bon dieu*)
1957	Search for a Method (*Question de méthode*)
1959	The Condemned of Altona (*Les Séquestrés d'Altona*)
1960	Critique of Dialectical Reason (*Critique de la raison dialectique*)
1963	The Words (*Les Mots*)

155 THE SECOND SEX

IN THE INTRODUCTION to her seminal feminist text, *The Second Sex*, Simone de Beauvoir states that woman *"is defined and differentiated with reference to man and not he with reference to her; she is the incidental, the inessential, as opposed to the essential. He is the Subject, he is the Absolute – she is the Other."*

To be a woman, then, is to be the Other of man. Beauvoir claimed that women have come to view themselves, and are viewed by men, as being naturally inferior to men. They tend to be confined to the domestic sphere, and defined by the passive and mundane tasks of their everyday existence.

Beauvoir identified what she called the myth of *"the eternal feminine,"* which functions to identify the woman as Other with the meaning of womanhood itself, to the extent that women see themselves through the myth of the eternal feminine and will often be complicit in their own subjugation. In order to throw off their status as Other, women must discard those illusions of womanhood that confine them to lives of endless repetition, passivity and drudgery. (*See* Simone de Beauvoir p40)

156 FAST FACT...

"It is nonsense to assert that revelry, vice, ecstasy, passion, would become impossible if man and woman were equal in concrete matters" – Simone de Beauvoir (1908 –1986)

157 FAST FACT...

THE CONCEPT of the original position was first advanced by Hungarian economist John Harsanyi.

158 FAST FACT...

"The principles of justice are chosen behind a veil of ignorance." – John Rawls (1921–2002)

159 ORIGINAL POSITION

🎓 **THE ORIGINAL POSITION** is a thought experiment devised by John Rawls, which aims to uncover *"the totality of conditions which we are ready upon due reflection to recognize as reasonable in our conduct towards one another."*
In other words, an experiment to discover which basic principles are essential in creating an equal, rational and unprejudiced society.

It works by asking us to imagine that we are members of group of free and equal people charged with coming to an agreement about the principles of justice that should underpin a fair society. Crucially, we as participants have to do this from behind a *"veil of ignorance."* This means that we will have no knowledge of our class position or social status, whether we are intelligent, strong or talented in any way, what we believe about morality, the level of wealth of the society in which we live, and so on.

The idea of the veil of ignorance is to force people to think about issues of justice and fairness from a position of complete impartiality, without being influenced by any personal interests or biases. With these barriers removed, the planned society can be based upon principles that are fair and equal to all.

THE VEIL OF IGNORANCE

Imagine you are setting up a brand new civilization. You need to decide how society is to be governed with the help of the citizens, so you invite them to a conference. Together, you must decide how best to create an equal, rational and unprejudiced society. You must attempt to do this from behind the "veil of ignorance", without being influenced by notions of class, wealth, religion, background, education or physical strength. Consider your response to the following questions:

- How will material goods be divided between the population? Should everyone get a fair share, or should some receive more than others?

- How will you protect your civilization? When is military action justified?

- Will you allow people from other civilizations to join yours? Will they have to fulfill certain criteria before emigrating?

- What happens to the elderly and the sick? Should they receive free healthcare, or should they be required to pay for this service? What about those who are unable to pay?

- How will children be educated? Should they or their parents have to pay for schooling? Should everyone be allowed to go to university?

- What constitutes a crime? How will criminals be punished?

- What is the best way to avoid religious prejudice? Should everyone be allowed to worship in their own way, or should religion be banned entirely?

- Who will be in charge of society? Will you elect a president? How will you decide on a leader? Who will be allowed to vote?

- If people are unhappy, do they have the right to complain to the government?

- Should men and women be allowed to work in any profession they choose? So, could women join the army's front line, or men work as midwives?

These sorts of questions have divided civilizations for centuries – can there ever be such a thing as an equal, rational and unprejudiced society?

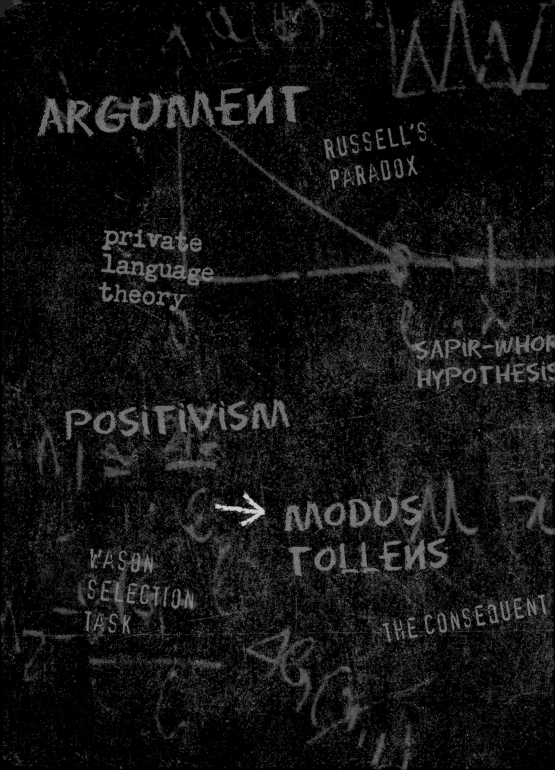

160 SYLLOGISMS

🎓 **A SYLLOGISM** is a form of inference from premises to conclusion. The classic example of a syllogism is:

- All men are mortal.
- Socrates is a man.
- Therefore, Socrates is mortal.

Here we have a major premise (*All men are mortal*), a minor premise (*Socrates is a man*), and a conclusion (*Socrates is mortal*). This can be represented abstractly as "*All M are P, S is M, Therefore S is P.*" All syllogisms of this form are deductively valid, which means that the conclusion necessarily follows the premises – if the premises are true, then the conclusion must also be true.

This is by no means the only valid syllogism, of course. Aristotle, who founded the discipline of formal logic, identified 256 forms of syllogism, of which 24 are valid (though there is some debate here).

161 FAST FACT...

📖 **ARISTOTLE** was the first to study the nature of deduction and to identify and formalize different sorts of syllogism.

Syllogisms are nothing like the last word in valid inference, and nowadays students of philosophy almost always study what is called "*First-order logic,*" which provides a more complete treatment of deductive systems of inference.

162 DEDUCTIVE AND INDUCTIVE ARGUMENTS

🎓 **A DEDUCTIVE ARGUMENT** is one where, given the truth of certain premises, it is possible to deduce (or infer) the truth of a conclusion. For example, the following syllogism is a deductive argument:

- No cows are grasshoppers.
- Daisy is a cow.
- Therefore, Daisy is not a grasshopper.

Here, the truth of the conclusion is guaranteed by the truth of the premises (assuming they are true).

An inductive argument does not provide such a guarantee, but rather provides support for a particular conclusion. So, for example, this is an inductive argument:

- One million clovers have been identified and catalogued.
- Each of them has three leaves.
- Therefore, all clovers have three leaves.

The existence of a million three-leaved clovers (in the absence of a four-leaved clover, for example) does provide *support* for the proposition that all clovers have three leaves, but it does not *guarantee* its truth, since it's always possible that a four-leaved clover will turn up.

Normally, but not always, deductive arguments move from the general to the particular, whereas inductive arguments move from the particular to the general (as in the case of our examples).

163 FAST FACT...

 **INDUCTIVE** reasoning is very useful for scientists, car mechanics, lawyers, doctors and anyone else who needs to interpret a large amount of data.

164 MODUS PONENS

MODUS PONENS, otherwise known as affirming the antecedent, is a simple and common type of valid argument. It has the following form:

- If P, then Q.
- P.
- Therefore, Q.

So, for example:

- If it is raining hard, the street will be wet.
- It's raining hard.
- Therefore, the street is wet.

This is a valid form of argument, since if the premises are true, then the conclusion must also be true. In our example, if it is true that the street will be wet if it's raining hard, and if it is also true that it is raining hard, then it necessarily follows that the street is wet.

165 FAST FACT...

"I approached the problem of induction through Hume. Hume, I felt, was perfectly right in pointing out that induction cannot be logically justified."
– Karl Popper (1902–1994)

166 FAST FACT...

IF TODAY is Wednesday, then Jane will play tennis. Today is Wednesday. Therefore, Jane will play tennis.
– An example of modus ponens.

167 MODUS TOLLENS

🎓 **MODUS TOLLENS**, sometimes known as denying the consequent, is the cousin of modus ponens. It has the following form:

- If P, then Q.
- Not Q.
- Therefore, not P.

So, using the same example:

- If it is raining hard, the street will be wet.
- The street is not wet.
- Therefore, it is not raining hard.

Clearly, this form of argument is also valid. If it is true that the street will be wet if it is raining hard, and if it is also true that the street is not wet, then it necessarily follows that it is not raining hard.

168 FAST FACT...

📖 **IF I AM** the getaway driver, then I can drive a car. I cannot drive a car. Therefore, I am not the getaway driver. – An example of modus tollens.

169 FAST FACT...

📖 **KARL POPPER**, who used modus tollens to support his arguments, grew up in 1920s Vienna, where he witnessed poverty and political upheaval.

170 AFFIRMING THE CONSEQUENT

🎓 **AFFIRMING THE CONSEQUENT** is a type of logical error that is closely related to the valid modus ponens form of argument. Its form is as follows:

- If P, then Q.
- Q.
- Therefore, P.

It is easy enough to see that this argument is not valid by once again using the wet street example:

- If it is raining hard, the street will be wet.
- The street is wet.
- Therefore, it is raining hard.

This time, the conclusion does not necessarily follow from the premises. The street might be wet because of a burst water pipe, for example, or because it is snowing.

171 FAST FACT...

📖 **IF I AM WATCHING** a scary movie, I feel scared. I feel scared. Therefore, I am watching a scary movie. – An example of affirming the consequent.

172 DENYING THE ANTECEDENT

DENYING THE ANTECEDENT is another type of logical error, but this time it is closely related to the valid modus tollens form of argument. It has the following form:

- If P, then Q.
- Not P.
- Therefore, not Q.

Again, it is easy to see that this argument is not valid:

- If it is raining hard, the street will be wet.
- It is not raining.
- Therefore, the street is not wet.

As before, the argument is invalid because the truth of the premises does not guarantee the truth of the conclusion. It is entirely possible that the street will be wet for a reason that has nothing to do with rain.

Both affirming the consequent and denying the antecedent are examples of formal logical errors.

173 FAST FACT...

📖 **IF A POODLE** is a breed of cat, then it is a mammal. A Poodle is not a breed of cat. Therefore, it is not a mammal. – An example of denying the antecedent.

174 FAST FACT...

📖 **ARTIFICIAL** intelligence pioneer Alan Turing once used a "denying the antecedent" argument to demonstrate that men might be machines.

175 VALID AND SOUND ARGUMENTS

🎓 **IT SHOULD BE CLEAR** by now that an argument is valid if, and only if, its conclusion is necessitated by its premises; or, to put it another way, if, and only if, the truth of its premises guarantees the truth of its conclusion.

A key point here is that it is perfectly possible for an argument to be valid, but for its conclusion to be false. Here is an example:

- All men are goats.
- Socrates is a man.
- Therefore, Socrates is a goat.

This syllogism is perfectly valid – if the premises are true, then the conclusion must be true – but complete nonsense, of course. In this case, it is easy to see that the conclusion is false because the major premise (*All men are goats*) is false.

An argument that is both valid and has true premises (and, therefore, a true conclusion) is termed a "sound" argument. Logic focuses on whether arguments are valid, rather than sound, but obviously if you are interested in the truth about things, you have got to be interested in the truth of premises and conclusions.

176 FAST FACT...

📖 **ALL TENNIS-PLAYING** dragons live in Bermuda. All humans are tennis-playing dragons. Therefore all humans live in Bermuda. – A valid argument, but not a sound one.

RIGHT: An illustration of the Tablet of Cebes. Cebes of Thebes was a disciple of Socrates and appears in Plato's *Phaedo*. The Tablet depicts the whole of human life and the various temptations that are put in our path.

La Séduction

177 FORMAL FALLACIES

A FORMAL FALLACY is a type of reasoning that is necessarily wrong because of some flaw in its logical structure. As we noted above, both affirming the consequent and denying the antecedent are examples of a formal fallacy. Other examples include: the fallacy of the undistributed middle; illicit major; illicit minor; and the fallacy of excluded premises.

An important point here is that it is entirely possible for an argument to be fallacious, and yet for its premises and conclusion to be true. Consider this argument, for example:

> • If global warming is occurring, then the polar ice caps will be melting.
> • The polar ice caps are melting.
> • Therefore, global warming is occurring.

The two premises are both true (arguably at least!), as is the conclusion. But the truth of the conclusion is not guaranteed by the truth of the premises (because something other than global warming might be causing the ice caps to melt). So the argument is fallacious – it is actually another example of affirming the consequent – despite having true premises and conclusion.

178 FAST FACT...

VAN GOGH was an artistic genius who died penniless. I am a penniless artist. Therefore I am a genius. – A famous example of a formal fallacy.

. . . .

🎓 **AN INFORMAL FALLACY** is an argument that is fallacious for reasons that are not related to its logical structure. Normally one can identify an informal fallacy by examining how an argument works. Consider the following example:

> • I have had experiences
> of the divine.
> Therefore, God exists.

This is an example of the fallacy of begging the question (which was first identified by Aristotle in his Prior Analytics). The premise assumes that there is such a thing as the divine, which is precisely what the argument is designed to demonstrate — namely, that God exists.

Here is another example of an informal fallacy:

God creating Adam

> • You can't have it both ways, a person's
> behavior is either a function of their genes
> or their environment.

This is a false dichotomy, which is the fallacy of assuming that there are only two options or alternatives on a particular issue, and that one cannot opt for both or some third option.

180 NECESSARY AND SUFFICIENT CONDITIONS

IMAGINE THAT you are investigating the causes of leukemia, and you identify a genetic fault that you think is implicated in the disease. This fault would be a *necessary condition* of the disease if it *had* to be present for the disease to occur (i.e. if the disease could not occur in its absence). It would be a *sufficient condition* of the disease if were true that every time it was present the disease occurred.

An important point here is that a condition can be necessary or sufficient without being the other. So, for example, exposure to radiation might be a necessary condition of getting sick with radiation poisoning, but it is not a sufficient condition (since it is possible to be exposed to small amounts of radiation without getting sick). Similarly, ingesting large amounts of alcohol might be a sufficient condition of intoxication, but it is not a necessary condition, since substances other than alcohol can cause intoxication.

181 FAST FACT...

IN ORDER for it to be true that James is an uncle, it is *necessary* that James (a) is male; (b) has or had a sibling; (c) has a nephew or niece.

182 FAST FACT...

KNOWING that it is true that James is an uncle is *sufficient* to know that he is male.

183 FAST FACT...

BEING A POODLE is *necessary but not sufficient* to being a dog.

184 FAST FACT...

"Today is 24th December" is necessary and sufficient for *"today is Christmas Eve"* (this is a necessary and sufficient condition).

185 POST HOC ERGO PROPTER HOC

🎓 **POST HOC ERGO PROPTER HOC**, which literally means *"after this, therefore because of this,"* is a common informal fallacy. It is the mistake of supposing that because some particular event occurred after another event, the first event must have been the cause of the second. This can be expressed formally as follows:

- A occurred,
- then B occurred.
- Therefore, A caused B.

It is very easy to find instances of this sort of fallacious reasoning. Consider, for example, the athlete who eats a particular breakfast before winning a race, and then reasons that he won because of the breakfast; or the person who decides the reason their cold got better was because they took a homeopathic remedy shortly before it began to clear up.

It is fairly obvious why this sort of reasoning is fallacious. There is no reason to suppose that the supposed effects of the first event would not have occurred in its absence. In other words, it is entirely possible that the athlete would have won the race and the person with the cold would have got better regardless of what they did beforehand.

186 FAST FACT...

📖 **THE LAWN IS WET.** If it rained last night, then it's unsurprising the lawn is wet. Therefore we can abduce it rained last night — abductive reasoning.

187 FAST FACT...

📖 **CHARLES SANDERS PEIRCE,** who introduced abduction into logic, was a prodigy who was studying chemistry at 8 and Kant's Critique of Pure Reason at 13.

188 FAST FACT...

📖 **PEIRCE** was truly prolific. His published output, on subjects ranging from mathematics to psychology, runs to 12,000 pages, with some 80,000 pages as yet unpublished.

189 RUSSELL'S PARADOX

🎓 **RUSSELL'S PARADOX,** which was first described by Bertrand Russell, requires some deep thought, but it is worth the effort, since it had large implications for the attempt to describe the foundations of mathematics at the beginning of the twentieth century. The paradox gets going by asking the following question:

190 FAST FACT...

📖 **RUSSELL'S PARADOX** might have been called Zermelo's paradox. German mathematician Ernst Zermelo discovered it a year earlier but did not publicize it.

Does the set of all sets that do not contain themselves as a member contain itself as a member?

Most sets do not contain themselves as a member. The set of all cars does not contain itself as a member, for example, because it is a set, not a car. But what about the set of all these sets that do not contain themselves as a member – does it contain itself as a member?

There is no possible answer to this question. If it does not contain itself as a member, then it is a set that does not contain itself as a member, so it should contain itself as a member (since it is the set of all sets that do not contain themselves as a member). But if it does contain itself as a member, then it is not a set that does not contain itself as a member, so it should not contain itself as a member.

191 FAST FACT...

📖 **BERTRAND RUSSELL** was a committed political activist, campaigning for civil rights and protesting against war and nuclear weapons.

And that, of course, is paradoxical.

192 SAPIR-WHORF HYPOTHESIS

THE SAPIR-WHORF linguistic relativity hypothesis, named after its originators, Edward Sapir and Benjamin Lee Whorf, holds that language determines how we perceive and think about the world and the objects it contains. In the words of Whorf:

"We dissect nature along the lines laid down by our native languages. The categories and types that we isolate from the world of phenomena we do not find there because they stare every observer in the face; on the contrary, the world is presented in a kaleidoscopic flux of impressions that has to be organized by our minds – and this means largely by the linguistic systems in our minds."

Thus, for example, Whorf notes that the Inuit Eskimos have some 20 words for snow, and he argues that this means they see snow differently than someone who lives in a country where snow is less prevalent.

193 FAST FACT...

BENJAMIN LEE WHORF (1897–1941) was originally a chemical engineer, who only took up linguistics as a hobby in the last 10 years of his life.

However, while it is probably true that language predisposes people to think in certain sorts of ways, there is little evidence to support the stronger view that language determines how we see and think about the world.

194 LOGICAL POSITIVISM

LOGICAL POSITIVISM is an approach to philosophy associated with the Vienna Circle of philosophers, including Rudolph Carnap and Otto Neurath, who met together in the early part of the twentieth century.

Its central claim is that statements are meaningful only to the extent that they are verifiable. A. J. Ayer put it this way:

> *"The criterion which we use to test the genuineness of apparent statements of fact is the criterion of verifiability. We say that a sentence is factually significant to any given person, if, and only if, he knows how to verify the proposition which it purports to express..."*

The consequence of this view is to render many sorts of statements – for example, religious, metaphysical and ethical statements – meaningless. Consider, for instance, the difficulty of figuring out how to verify statements such as *"God is love"* or *"Murder is wrong."*

195 FAST FACT...

MORITZ SCHLICK, founding father of logical positivism and the Vienna Circle, began his career as a physicist, studying under Max Planck.

Logical positivism, however, runs into one particular difficulty. It is not clear that the verification principle itself is verifiable. If it is not, then it seems that logical positivism is founded on a claim that is self-defeating.

The Natural History Museum in Vienna, Austria

196 WITTGENSTEIN'S PICTURE THEORY OF LANGUAGE

🎓 **WITTGENSTEIN'S** first great work of philosophy was *Tractatus Logico-Philosophicus*, in which he set out his picture theory of language.

It was Wittgenstein's view that the world is made up of facts – the existence of states of affair – and that the propositions of language depict those facts, which means that the logical structure of language mirrors the logical structure of the world. Thus, for example, whether a proposition such as *"The cat is on the mat"* is true depends on whether the state of affair obtains in the world.

Wittgenstein argued that all statements that are not reducible to this basic form are nonsense, which has the somewhat disconcerting consequence that most of philosophy, including the *Tractatus* itself, is nonsense. As he put it:

> *"My propositions serve as elucidations in the following way: anyone who understands me eventually recognizes them as nonsensical, when he has used them – as steps – to climb up beyond them."*

The final statement of the Tractatus provides a neat summary of Wittgenstein's early philosophical position: *"Whereof we cannot speak, thereof we must remain silent."*

---

197 FAST FACT...

📖 **WITTGENSTEIN** dismissed logical positivism as a gross misreading of the *Tractatus*, and took to reading poetry during meetings of the Vienna Circle.

198 FAST FACT...

📖 *"The human body is the best picture of the human soul "*
– Ludwig Wittgenstein (1809 1951)

199 WITTGENSTEIN'S PRIVATE LANGUAGE ARGUMENT

🎓 **IN PHILOSOPHICAL INVESTIGATIONS**, the great work of the second part of his career, Wittgenstein asks whether we could imagine a language in which a person could name their inner experiences so that another person could not understand the language. The answer he gives in the section of this work now known as "the private language argument" is that such language is not possible.

Unfortunately, Wittgenstein's argument against the possibility of a private language is complex and unsystematic, which means summarizing it is fraught with danger. However, it is perhaps fair to say that its major claim is that language is only meaningful in the context of a framework of rules that are necessarily public, which makes a private language impossible.

Why do the rules of language have to be public? Well, consider how you might go about establishing a connection between the word "chow" and a stomach pain you periodically experience. The problem is that you can never be sure you're applying the word in the correct context. Telling yourself that the pain you're experiencing this time is the same sort of pain as last time isn't good enough, because memory is unreliable. There is no "criterion of correctness" in terms of which the word might be meaningful.

200 FAST FACT...

📖 **IN 1982**, American philosopher Saul Kripke published a critique of the private language argument. Some said he misrepresented Wittgenstein, and referred to his account as "Kripkenstein."

201 THE TWIN EARTH THOUGHT EXPERIMENT

🎓 **THE TWIN EARTH THOUGHT EXPERIMENT,** which was created by Hilary Putnam, has the following form.

202 FAST FACT...

📖 **HILARY PUTNAM** is known for the intense scrutiny he applies to his own arguments, often exposing flaws in them and being forced to change his position.

Imagine a planet that is identical to the Earth in every respect (including the people who inhabit it) except one: on "Twin Earth," the liquid called "water" has the chemical composition H_2OXYZ rather than H_2O. Imagine also a time before the inhabitants of Earth and Twin Earth had any way of knowing about the chemical composition of the liquids they call "water," so the experience of "water" is identical on both planets.

In this situation, the question arises of whether an inhabitant of Earth and their twin on Twin Earth mean the same thing when they refer to "water." Putnam argues that they do not, but the difference in the meaning of water and "water" cannot be anything to do with what is in the brains of the speakers, since these are identical. From this it follows that "'meanings' just ain't in the head."

203 COGNITIVE BIASES

MOST OF US like to think that we are not particularly prone to irrationality. We accept that we will make occasional mistakes, of course, but do not want to think that we do so in a systematic or predictable fashion. Unfortunately, there is plenty of evidence to suggest that we are probably more optimistic than we ought to be in this respect.

Cognitive biases are systematic mistakes in reasoning and judgement that in various ways tend to reflect the interests and experiences of the person making the mistakes. So, for example, *self-serving bias* refers to our propensity to attribute our successes to intrinsic personality factors and our failures to external situational factors. The *primacy effect* refers to a propensity to assign more weight to the things we learn early about a phenomenon than the things we learn later (though this is complicated by the existence of a recency effect).

The importance of cognitive bias is partly that it undermines our ability to make decisions on rational, evidential grounds.

204 CONFIRMATION BIAS

CONFIRMATION BIAS refers to our tendency to favor information or evidence that supports our already-existing beliefs and hypotheses. In a classic study, the psychologists Albert Hastorf and Hadley Cantril showed students from Princeton and Dartmouth a football game between their two colleges. They found a strong tendency for the students to assess the game through the filter of their prior commitments. For example, Princeton students saw double the number of infringements on the part of Dartmouth players as the Dartmouth students saw.

Confirmation bias has large implications for the way in which we practice science. In particular, it puts a premium on the development of alternative hypotheses, since this decreases the chances of people becoming attached to their "pet" hypotheses, and on attempts to falsify rather than confirm hypotheses.

205 FAST FACT...

📖 **AMOS TVERSKY**, co-discoverer of cognitive bias, was a captain in the Israel Defence Force and was decorated for bravery.

206 FAST FACT...

📖 **TVERSKY'S PARTNER**, Daniel Kahneman, who is also Jewish, spent his childhood on the run from the Nazis in wartime France.

207 WASON SELECTION TASK

👨‍🎓 **THERE ARE FOUR CARDS** in front of you. The first shows a square; the second, a circle; the third, the color yellow; the fourth, the color red. You know for certain that each card has a shape on one side and a color on the other.

Your job is to turn over only those cards necessary to ensure that the following rule has been upheld in the production of the cards.

> If a card has a circle on one side, then it has the color yellow on the other side.

Which cards should you turn over?

This task is known as the Wason selection task, and we are incredibly bad at it. It seems simple, but only some 20% of people who complete this task get it right. The right answer is that you need to turn over the circle (to make sure it has the color yellow on the other side) and the red card (to make sure it doesn't have a circle on the other side).

208 FAST FACT...

📖 **PETER CATHCART WASON,** the cognitive psychologist who created the Wason Selection Task, was also an International Master in correspondence chess.

One of the most famous selection tasks in literature occurs in Shakespeare's The Merchant of Venice. Potential suitors must choose between three metal caskets to win Portia's hand in marriage.

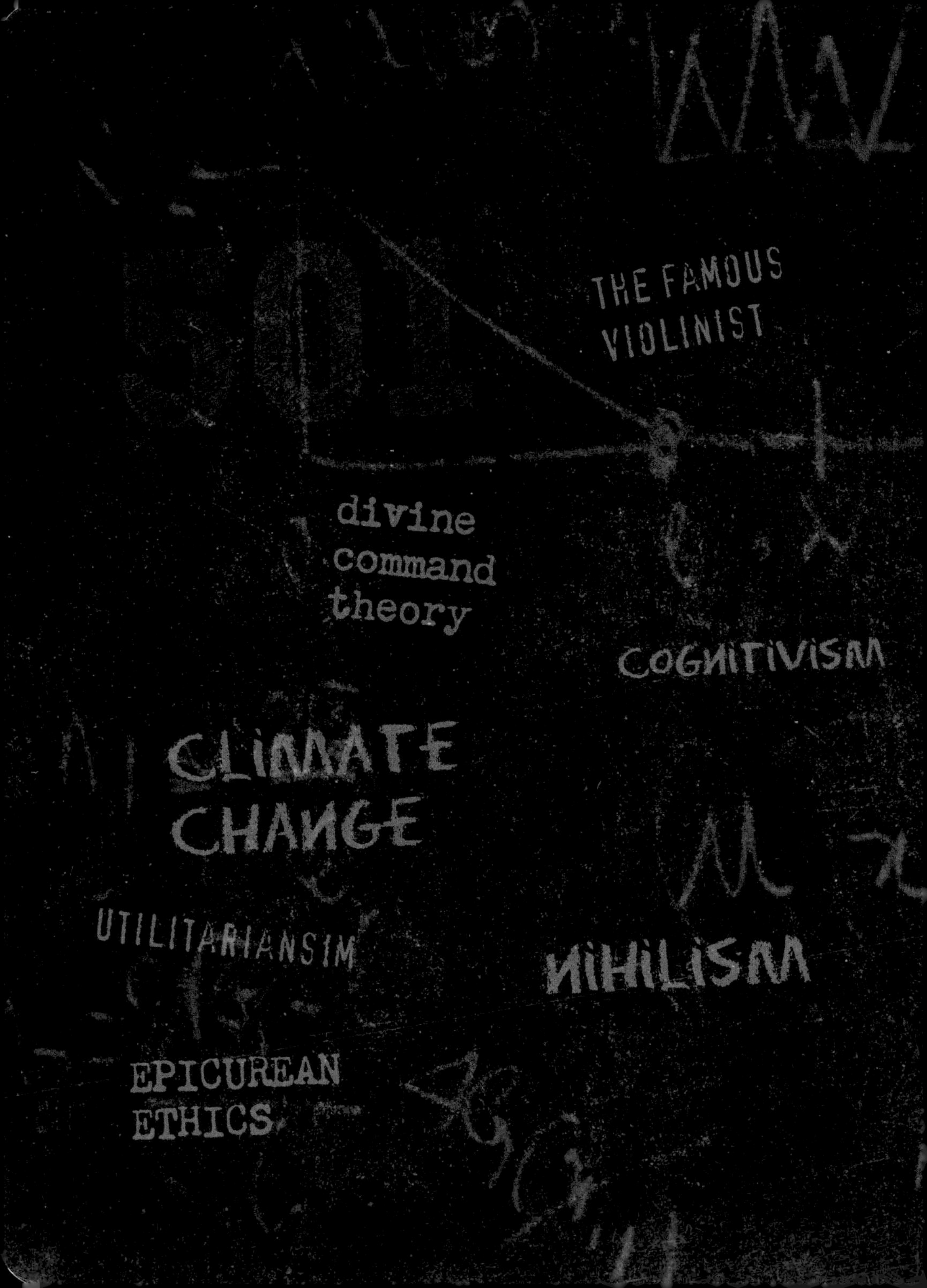

THE FAMOUS
VIOLINIST

divine
command
theory

COGNITIVISM

CLIMATE
CHANGE

UTILITARIANSIM

NIHILISM

EPICUREAN
ETHICS

META-ETHICS

STOICISM

→ Ethics ↙

LYING   VITIMIZATION

                    ABORTION

IS/OUGHT
GAP

personhood   VIRTUE

209 META-ETHICS

CONSIDER THE FOLLOWING scenario. Your spouse is dying, and can only be saved by a drug that is sold for $20,000 in a single store. You cannot possibly afford this, so you go to the store owner and ask whether you can pay in installments. He refuses, despite the fact he would make a large profit on the drug if he accepted your terms. You are so desperate for the medication that you consider breaking in and stealing it.

If your first reaction to this scenario (owed to Lawrence Kohlberg) is to think in a general sense about the nature of right and wrong, the meaning of moral claims, and so on, rather than about whether it would be morally permissible to steal the drug in this precise situation, then you are thinking about meta-ethics.

210 FAST FACT...

📖 **AUSTRALIAN** philosopher J. L. Mackie (1917–1981), famous for his views on meta-ethics, believed that there are no objective values.

Meta-ethics is the domain of ethics that deals with questions such as *"Do moral facts exist?"* and *"What is the meaning of a judgement that something is right or wrong?"* Philosophers have always discussed these sorts of questions, but it is only in the last 100 years that they have been considered in a systematic manner.

211 NON-COGNITIVISM VERSUS COGNITIVISM

NON-COGNITIVISM is a meta-ethical position which holds that moral statements cannot be true or false in the same way as a proposition such as "The cat sat on the mat" can be. Non-cognitivists are committed to the view that there are no moral facts in the world waiting to be discovered. There are a number of varieties of non-cognitivism. The British philosopher A. J. Ayer favored an approach termed *emotivism*, which, broadly speaking, sees moral statements as expressing an emotion. So saying *"Giving to charity is right"* is a bit like saying *"Hooray for giving to charity!"*

212 FAST FACT...

BRITISH philosopher G. E. Moore, a proponent of moral cognitivism, stated that *"goodness is a simple, undefinable, non-natural property."* He called this position *"ethical non-naturalism."*

Cognitivism, in contrast, asserts that moral claims involve propositions that can be true or false. Some, but not all, cognitivists think there are such things as moral facts, in light of which it is possible to make objective judgements about people's actions. This idea is sometimes called *moral realism*.

It is also possible for cognitivism to be anti-realist about moral facts. Error theory, for example, asserts that while all moral claims are *"truth-apt"* (i.e. they express propositions that can be true or false), it is in fact the case that all such claims are false.

213 FAST FACT...

BRITISH philosopher A. J. Ayer was an MI6 agent during World War II.

214 FAST FACT...

"There is philosophy, which is about conceptual analysis — about the meaning of what we say — and there is all of this ... all of life."
– A. J. Ayer (1910–1989)

215 NORMATIVE ETHICS

🎓 **NORMATIVE ETHICS** is the branch of ethics that deals with the question of how people ought to behave. So, for example, if you are weighing up the moral arguments for and against abortion, you are doing normative ethics. There are three main normative ethical approaches: consequentialist ethics; deontological ethics; and virtue ethics.

Consequentialist approaches judge whether an action is right or wrong by looking at its outcome. For example, it might be held that an action is right to the extent that it promotes the greatest happiness of the greatest number of people. Deontological approaches, in contrast, emphasize the importance of binding moral norms. It is entirely possible for an action with good consequences to be prohibited, since what counts is whether the action is in accordance with the requisite moral norm. The virtue ethics approach differs from the first two in being not so much concerned with actions as with character. People should behave in ways that cultivate a virtuous character, rooted in traits such as honesty, empathy and courage.

Medieval chivalric code emphasized the importance of virtuous behavior.

216 MORAL RELATIVISM

🎓 **MORAL RELATIVISM**, as a meta-ethical position, is the idea that moral claims are not true in some sort of objective, universal sense, but rather true in relation to the culture, traditions and values of some particular group. A moral relativist will accept that moral claims are truth-apt (they involve propositions that can be true or false) but will deny that there are universal standards against which their truth can be established.

Few philosophers will admit to being moral relativists because the position inevitably raises the worrying possibility that behavior most of us would consider to be morally repugnant, for example slavery or child marriage, might be entirely unproblematic or praiseworthy within the culture of a particular society.

However, moral relativism does accurately describe the widespread moral disagreements that exist between cultures and in this respect it can be very useful.

217 FAST FACT...

📖 *"The moral order ... is just as much part of the fundamental nature of the universe ... as is the axioms of geometry or arithmetic."*
– Scottish philosopher W. D. Ross

Moral relativism may be able to help balance moral views of different societies

218 NIHILISM

 **THE TERM NIHILISM** first came into widespread use in the mid-nineteenth century, referring to a Russian revolutionary movement that rejected all forms of authority and advocated violence as a mechanism of political change. However, it wasn't long before the term began to be used in the way that it is understood today, namely, to refer to the view that there is no such thing as right and wrong (and also to refer to the despair that people feel when confronted by a meaningless world).

Friedrich Niezsche is perhaps the most significant philosopher to have made use of the notion of nihilism. He used the term to describe the vacuum that is left in moral order with the disintegration of Christianity and the increasing awareness that all our value systems are human creations. However, there are also echoes of nihilism in more contemporary approaches to moral philosophy. Error theory, for example, to the extent that it holds that value systems are built out of moral propositions that are necessarily false, teeters on the edges of nihilism.

Nihilism has been used to desribe the sense of despair that we feel in a world that is apparently without meaning.

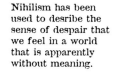

219 FAST FACT...

 THE TERM nihilism was coined by the German philosopher Friedrich Heinrich Jacobi (1743–1819).

220 IS/OUGHT GAP

🎓 **A CLAIM** that is often made in a discussion about the morality of same-sex relationships is that homosexual behavior is wrong because it is unnatural. This is a bad argument, which can be simply demonstrated by means of a couple of examples:

- Skydiving is unnatural, therefore it is morally wrong.

- Abstaining from sex is unnatural, therefore those Catholic priests who manage to abstain from sex are immoral.

- Heart pacemakers are unnatural, therefore, their use to save lives is immoral.

The argument does not work due to what is called the "Is/Ought Gap," which was first noted by David Hume. Simply put, there is a logical disconnect between the way the world is and the way people believe it *ought* to be. So, for example, if it transpired that human beings were innately predisposed to murder and mayhem, this would tell us nothing about how we *ought* to behave. If it is wrong to kill people, the fact that killing might be natural is neither here nor there. Hume's reasoning called into question the validity of "ought" statements and the foundations upon which moral judgements are made.

221 ARISTOTLE'S ETHICS

ARISTOTLE'S FAMOUS DOCTRINE of the "golden mean" is central to his thoughts about ethics and virtue. He argues that human happiness is dependent on cultivating the excellence of our rational soul. In ethical terms, this means charting a course between inappropriate excess and deficiency, while remaining sensitive to the demands of the particular situations we are in. Thus, for example, courage lies on the "mean" between extremes of cowardice on the one hand and rashness on the other.

Aristotle's approach does not provide a shopping list of right actions. There is no generally applicable formula to which we can refer to determine the right action in any particular situation. Rather, virtue consists in thinking well (because we are by nature rational animals), which in turn involves soberly weighing up the choices we have in particular situations, and then choosing in a way that will maximize the excellence of our souls.

Aristotle's discussion on ethics is the earliest fully developed expression of a virtue ethics approach. For him, the foundation of ethics was choosing to live well.

222 FAST FACT...

ARISTOTLE'S ethics later influenced the work of Avicenna, Averroes, Maimonidies and Thomas Aquinas, as well as many modern philosophers.

Hmmm...

223 FAST FACT...

"We are not studying in order to know what virtue is, but to become good, for otherwise there would be no profit in it." – Aristotle

224 EPICUREAN ETHICS

ACCORDING to the Ancient Greek philosopher Epicurus, pleasure is the primary good.

> "...we call pleasure the alpha and omega of a happy life. Pleasure is our first and kindred good. It is the starting-point of every choice and of every aversion, and to it we come back, inasmuch as we make feeling the rule by which to judge of every good thing."

However, despite the accusations of his contemporaries to the contrary, Epicurus was not a hedonist, rejecting the idea that we should actively pursue the fleshy excitement of sex, drugs and rock 'n' roll. Instead, he argued that our happiness was best secured by a life of friendship and quiet contemplation. It was his view that pleasures rooted in strong desires will inevitably be destructive, since they are inextricably linked to pain and frustration. Therefore, the sensible course is to seek bodily and psychological equilibrium, where restless desire is minimized.

225 FAST FACT...

EPICURUS taught that pleasure and pain are the measures of what is good and evil.

226 FAST FACT...

THE EPICUREAN emphasis on minimizing harm and maximizing happiness influenced the democratic thinkers of the French Revolution, as well as John Locke.

227 DIVINE COMMAND THEORY

🎓 **DIVINE COMMAND THEORY** holds that things are morally good or bad, and actions are obligatory, permissible or forbidden, purely because of God's will or commands. Matthew's Gospel provides a nice example of what a divine command looks like:

Thou shalt love the Lord thy God with all thy heart, and with all thy soul, and with all thy mind. This is the first and great commandment. And the second is like unto it, Thou shalt love thy neighbor as thyself.

The binding character of divine commands is a function of God's sovereignty. God is the creator of all things, the supreme, omnipotent Being, which means that his authority is absolute. If he commands you to sacrifice your son, then it is obligatory that you do so; if he tells you to stay away from your neighbor's ox, then you need to leave that ox alone.

One major flaw of Divine Command Theory is that it presupposes God's existence. This was uncontentious in the Middle Ages, but is hugely contentious in the present day.

An illustration depicting the demon Mephisopheles in front of God and the three archangels (1874)

228 STOICISM

ACCORDING to the Stoics, the world is governed by a divine plan, which works in never-ending cycles of life and destruction. This explains why the stoics believed that we should approach fortune and misfortune in exactly the same way: anything that happens to us is just part of the unfolding of a divine plan that is beyond our power to influence and is ultimately good.

229 FAST FACT...

ZENO of Citium, founder of the Stoics, arrived in Athens by accident after surviving a shipwreck.

230 FAST FACT...

THE CRATER Zeno on the Moon is named in honor of Zeno of Citium.

A stoic analogy that makes this point involves a dog tied to the back of a wagon. When the wagon moves, the dog can either pull against it, thereby strangling itself, or it can calmly go along with it. The dog will be heading off with the wagon no matter what it chooses to do – the only real choice consists in how it deals with what's happening. As the stoic philosopher and Roman statesman Marcus Aurelius continually remarked, we control only our own opinions and attitudes, and here alone virtue is possible. A good or virtuous man, then, accepts his lot, whatever it might be, in the knowledge that whatever life brings us, it could not have been otherwise.

231 FAST FACT...

WHILE studying under the Cynic Crates of Thebes, Zeno was made to carry a pot of lentil soup around Athens. Crates then smashed the pot, splattering Zeno with soup.

232 JEREMY BENTHAM'S UTILITARIANISM

UTILITARIANISM, a form of consequentialism, has its origins in the ideas of Jeremy Bentham. He argued that the wellspring of human activity is a desire to experience pleasure and avoid pain. It follows, then, that the key to happiness is ensuring that you have as much pleasure and as little pain as possible. Bentham turns this idea into a moral theory, arguing that actions should aim at achieving as great a balance of pleasure over pain as possible for the greatest number of people. This is Bentham's "Greatest Happiness Principle."

233 FAST FACT...

AS A toddler, Jeremy Bentham was found sitting on his father's desk reading a multi-volume history of England.

"By the principle of utility is meant that principle which approves or disapproves of every action whatsoever, according to the tendency which it appears to have to augment or diminish the happiness of the party whose interest is in question."

In order to determine how to act in any particular situation, we need to perform a *"hedonic calculus,"* which involves summing all the values of all the pleasures on one side, and those of all the pains on the other. If the balance is on the side of pleasure, then you know the act is moral.

234 FAST FACT...

BENTHAM spent 16 years designing a prison he called a Panopticon. The idea was to have a building where inmates could be watched without them realizing.

235 FAST FACT...

"Nature has placed mankind under the governance of two sovereign masters, pain and pleasure. It is for them alone to point out what we ought to do..." – Jeremy Bentham

236 J. S. MILL'S UTILITARIANISM

BENTHAM'S version of utilitarianism is haunted by a rather troubling thought. Suppose it turns out that human beings are at their happiest while indulging in debauched pleasures of the flesh. If we are only interested in the quantity of pleasure in achieving the greatest balance of pleasure over pain, then it seems that utilitarianism might require that we spend all our time enjoying wild parties.

This possibility was a bit much for J. S. Mill's Victorian sensibility, so he was led to argue that it is possible to distinguish between higher and lower pleasures. Not surprisingly, it was Mill's argument that higher pleasures, which are associated with the higher faculties, are the superior kind. As he memorably put it, it's better to be Socrates dissatisfied than a pig satisfied.

Mill's argument in favor of the superiority of the higher pleasures is simply that you do not find any people who are able to enjoy both higher and lower pleasures expressing a preference for the latter.

237 FAST FACT...

JAMES MILL aimed to create in his son a genius intellect who would carry on the cause of utilitarianism after he and Bentham had died.

238 FAST FACT...

"It is better to be a human dissatisfied than a pig satisfied."
– J S Mill (1806–1873)

239 FAST FACT...

AFTER Bentham's death, his head and skeleton were preserved and dressed in his clothes. The Auto-icon, as it is known, is kept on display at University College London (UCL).

240 FAST FACT...

FOR SPECIAL anniversaries, the Auto-icon is brought to meetings of UCL's College Council, where it is listed as "present but not voting."

241 TORTURE AND THE TICKING BOMB

🎓 WRITING in the *New Republic* in September 2002, the legal scholar Richard Posner claimed that that *"If torture is the only means of obtaining the information necessary to prevent the detonation of a nuclear bomb in Times Square, torture should be used – and will be used – to obtain the information."*

The sort of situation that Posner is imagining is known as a "ticking bomb scenario." It aims to show that there are circumstances in which just about everybody will agree that torture is justified. Its basic structure is simple: some large harm is about to occur and you need a crucial piece of information to have a chance of preventing it. The person who you think knows the information refuses to speak; if you torture him, there is a chance he will talk. Torture causes harm, but vastly less harm than will occur if you do not find out what you need to know. Therefore, in this sort of situation, torture is morally permissible (and perhaps obligatory).

Vintage engraving showing a scene from 19th Century London, England. Prisoners walk round the exercise yard at Newgate Prison, circa 1870.

242 THE PROBLEM OF VICTIMIZATION

IMAGINE that there has been a brutal murder in a particular town. The police are certain it was just a random attack, but it has led to an outbreak of vigilantism, which has seen members of a vulnerable minority scapegoated and attacked. It so happens there is a person living in the area who has a prior conviction for violence. He has served his time, and the police know he isn't responsible for the murder. However, they also know that if they plant incriminating evidence against him, they'll be able to secure his conviction.

The worry about this sort of scenario is the possibility that utilitarianism will justify framing the innocent man. The outbreak of vigilantism would likely die down, which in turn would end the scapegoating of the vulnerable minority, and thereby promote the greatest balance of happiness over unhappiness. Therefore, it would follow that in utilitarian terms, framing the man is justified, a conclusion that many people, including some utilitarians, will find highly counterintuitive.

243 ACT UTILITARIANISM VERSUS RULE UTILITARIANISM

A POSSIBLE escape from the problem of victimization lies in the distinction between "act utilitarianism" and "rule utilitarianism." Broadly speaking, the former looks at the effects of particular acts in determining right and wrong, whereas the latter looks at the effects of following particular rules.

A rule utilitarian might accept that specific acts of victimization will probably result in an increase of general happiness. However, they can argue that this does not justify the practice of victimization, since if it were instantiated as a rule for action, the effect would be negative in terms of the general happiness balance. So, for example, they might argue that the problem with framing people for crimes is that it would undermine people's confidence in the justice system, because inevitably it wouldn't be possible to keep the practice secret.

However, as always, there are further complications. Part of the problem with rule utilitarianism is that it risks collapsing back into act utilitarianism. Rules will tend to become so specific that they end up describing specific acts.

244 KANT'S CATEGORICAL IMPERATIVE

🎓 **IMMANUEL KANT** rejected the idea that acting morally involves looking at situations, weighing up consequences, and determining which acts would produce the best outcomes. Instead, he argued in favor of deontological ethics, which holds that that acting morally is a matter of acting in accordance with a binding moral law. This law is categorical in nature, which means it can be expressed in the form of commands such as "Do this" and "Don't do that."

More specifically, Kant identified what he called a "categorical imperative." Through this it is possible to determine whether an act is permissible. Categorical imperative has the following form:

"Act only in accordance with that maxim through which you can at the same time will that it become a universal law."

Roughly speaking, what this means is that you are only acting morally if, and only if, it is possible to universalize the maxim, or principle, governing your action so that it could function as a universal law governing the actions of everybody who happens to be in the same situation as you. If you cannot universalize it, the act is immoral, and you need to refrain from doing it.

245 FAST FACT...

📖 **IN METAPHYSICS** of Ethics (1797), Kant places reason as the fundamental authority for morality.

246 FAST FACT...

📖 **"A METAPHYSICS** of morals is ... necessary ... because morals ... remain subject to all sorts of corruption as long as we are without that clue ... by which to appraise them correctly." – Immanuel Kant (1724–1804)

247 KANT ON LYING

TO ILLUSTRATE what the idea of the categorical imperative involves, Kant used the example of lying to a friend to get a loan. Let us assume that lying to a friend implies the principle that you should lie if it helps you to get what you want. Kant argues that such a principle cannot be universalized, because it is self-defeating. If people simply lied whenever they wanted something, the whole idea of promising or giving one's word would disappear. Nobody would ever believe promises, so there would be no point in promising; lying would have no effect because nobody would ever believe the lie in the first place.

Therefore, universalizing the maxim of your action, when that action involves lying, results in a contradiction. According to Kant, this means we have a "perfect duty" to refrain from acting in terms of the maxim since it cannot be willed as a universal law. It follows, then, that it is never permissible to lie to a friend to secure a loan.

248 ELIZABETH ANSCOMBE AND VIRTUE ETHICS

IN 1958 the English philosopher Elizabeth Anscombe published an article entitled "Modern Moral Philosophy," which has been credited with sparking a revival of interest in virtue ethics. The major thesis of the article is that the time has come to jettison concepts such as moral obligation, moral right and moral wrong, since these only make sense within religious frameworks that are no longer generally accepted.

249 FAST FACT...

ELIZABETH ANSCOMBE, a devout Roman Catholic, defended the Church's opposition to contraception and was twice arrested while protesting against abortion.

Instead, moral philosophy should focus on issues to do with character, and particularly the virtues that are linked to human flourishing. Virtue is not a matter of a hedonic calculus or dutiful behavior, but is rather about cultivating the right character traits. Proper normative ethics requires that we engage with the *character* of the moral agent, something that is almost entirely missing from other approaches.

250 FAST FACT...

ANSCOMBE attracted controversy for her public opposition to Britain's entry into World War II.

251 FAST FACT...

IT HAS been suggested that Anscombe's 1948 demolition of C. S. Lewis's theory of naturalism was so humiliating that he gave up philosophy and turned to writing children's literature.

252   PREFERENCE UTILITARIANISM

IN CONTRAST to classical utilitarianism, which identifies happiness as the locus of moral value, preference utilitarianism holds that good actions should aim at the satisfaction of preferences, even those preferences that do not increase aggregate or total happiness. This position is perhaps most notably associated with Peter Singer, who argues that an action is right to the extent that it increases the ability of any beings affected by it to satisfy their preferences.

This view leads to a number of very tricky philosophical issues. Suppose, for example, a baby is born with severe brain damage. In this situation, the baby might lack the cognitive apparatus necessary to have preferences at all. It is likely that it would have little, if any, sense of self and no cognitive or emotional investment in its own survival. In this situation, it is not at all clear that the infant has a life that is worth living, or that by ending its life we would be depriving it of the ability to satisfy its preferences. It is Singer's view that it could be possible to justify ending the life of a severely brain damaged baby (assuming the consent of the parents had been obtained), a view that many find controversial.

253   FAST FACT...

📖 **PETER SINGER'S** parents were Viennese Jews, who emigrated to Australia in 1938. Three of his grandparents died in Nazi concentration camps.

254   FAST FACT...

📖 **SINGER'S** *Animal Liberation* (1975) was a major influence on the modern animal rights movement.

255   FAST FACT...

📖 *"The only legitimate boundary to our concern for the interests of other beings is the point at which it is no longer accurate to say that the other being has interests."* – Peter Singer

256 ABORTION AND PERSONHOOD

🎓 **THE DEBATE** about the ethics of abortion is often fought over the question of whether a fetus is a person (primarily due to the notion that human beings only have the kinds of lives worth living if they are persons). Thus, Peter Singer has argued that as a fetus lacks attributes such as rationality, self-consciousness and awareness, its life has no intrinsic value, and therefore abortion is morally permissible.

257 FAST FACT...

📖 **JUDITH JARVIS THOMSON** was born in New York City to a Jewish father and a Catholic mother. Judith converted to Judaism aged 14.

However, the argument over personhood is complicated by two main problems. Firstly, there is no consensus amongst philosophers about which attributes have to be in place for personhood to exist, or whether (and if so, at what point in its development) a fetus possesses these attributes. Secondly, there is the worry that certain human beings (for example, newly born infants or patients in a coma) also lack the attributes of personhood, and yet we do not tend to think that deliberately ending their lives would be morally permissible.

258 FAST FACT...

📖 **IN HER PAPER** "A Defense of Abortion," Thomson states: "*the right to life consists not in the right not to be killed, but rather in the right not to be killed unjustly.*"

259 THE FAMOUS VIOLINIST

JUDITH JARVIS THOMSON asks us to consider the following scenario. You wake up in the morning and find yourself in a hospital bed attached to an unconscious famous violinist. He has a fatal kidney ailment, and it turns out that you alone have the right blood type to help. You have been kidnapped and your circulatory system has been plugged into his. You are told that you cannot be unplugged, since the violinist will die if that happens. The good news, though, is that you only have to stay attached for nine-months, after which time the violinist will be well enough to survive on his own. So, are you morally obligated to stay attached?

This thought experiment is designed to challenge the assumption that if a fetus is a person, then abortion is morally wrong. Thomson argues that there is no moral obligation for you to stay attached to the violinist, since you have rights that trump the violinist's right to life. By analogy, abortion is morally permissible, since a woman's right to control what happens to her own body is more important than a fetus's right to life (assuming that it has such a right).

260 MERE ADDITION PARADOX

🎓 **THE MERE ADDITION** paradox arises from the idea that lives that are barely worth living are nevertheless still worth living. This results in what Derek Parfit called "the repugnant conclusion:"

For any possible population of at least ten billion people, all with a very high quality of life, there must be some much larger imaginable population whose existence, if other things are equal, would be better even though its members have lives that are barely worth living.

The precise argument to support this conclusion is a little complex, but it is easy enough to get a sense of it. The key point is that if you think that total happiness is what is morally important, then if you get enough people who are barely happy, at some point you will end up with what looks like a better society than one populated with a smaller number of people who are very happy.

This is highly counterintuitive but the conclusion is hard to avoid, and the issues suggesting the repugnant conclusion are still very much alive in the field of population ethics.

261 FAST FACT...

📖 *"My life seemed like a glass tunnel, through which I was moving faster every year, and at the end of which there was darkness."*
– Derek Parfit's description of his life before he lost the conception of a separate self.

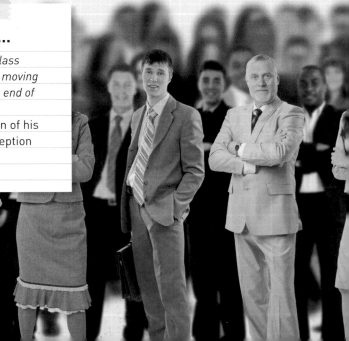

🎓 **JOSHUA KNOBE,** one of the leading lights of experimental philosophy, describes the rationale of the approach as follows:

At the heart of this new field is the idea that we can make progress on many of the age-old questions of philosophy – about ethics, politics, language – if we can come to a better understanding of the way people's minds work. To aid in this endeavor, experimental philosophers actually go out and conduct experimental studies that examine the way people think about various matters of philosophical importance.

So, for example, an experimental philosopher interested in free will and determinism might conduct a series of experiments to determine whether people are more inclined towards compatibilist or incompatibilist positions.

The field of experimental philosophy is only a few years old, but already hundreds of papers have been published, conferences have been held, and the work of experimental philosophers has been featured in mainstream publications such as *The New York Times*.

263 CLIMATE CHANGE AND CAUSAL INEFFICACY

🎓 **LET US ASSUME** that androgenic climate change is real, and that its consequences will be devastating for people living in the future. At least arguably, it would seem to follow that each of us are morally obliged to take reasonable steps to minimize our contribution to the sorts of things that cause climate change, perhaps taking fewer transatlantic flights or burning less fossil fuel.

However, the philosopher James Garvey has identified a difficulty with this argument, which he calls the "problem of causal inefficacy." If androgenic climate change is caused by the actions of a vast number of people, then it seems to follow that the contribution of any particular person to climate change is so small as to be irrelevant. In other words, if one subtracted their contribution from the causal story of climate change, the world would be left just as it is. If that is correct, then no particular person causes morally relevant harm, which means there is no obligation on the part of individual people to alter their behavior.

264 THE 'YUK-FACTOR'

JIM AND JUNE are siblings. One night a long time ago while on vacation they made an informed choice to have sex with each other. The following things are true about what happened: they knew that June could not get pregnant because of a medical condition; they have never repeated the event; they have never regretted it; they have never told anybody else about what happened and they never will; they still regard it as an entirely positive experience.

> Did they behave immorally in having sex with each other?

If people are asked about scenarios such as this one, which involve the violation of a strong social norm, but which on the face of it are harmless, private and consensual, they tend to claim the behavior described is immoral, but they are unable to offer substantive reasons for their judgement. This suggests that at least part of what is going on when people make moral judgements is non-rational and emotional.

This carries obvious dangers. If we are simply reacting to behavior on the basis of a "yuk-factor," then we run the risk of condemning people just because we find them or their behavior distasteful, not because we have good, rational grounds for doing so.

265 FAST FACT...

📖 *"For no one by the law of nature is bound to ... hold anything to be good or evil, but what he himself ... pronounces to be so."* – Baruch Spinoza (1632–1677)

Yuk!

SEXUAL
POLITICS

501

conservativism

LIBERTARIANISM

ANARCHISM

FEMINISM

speciesism

RIGHTS OF
MAN

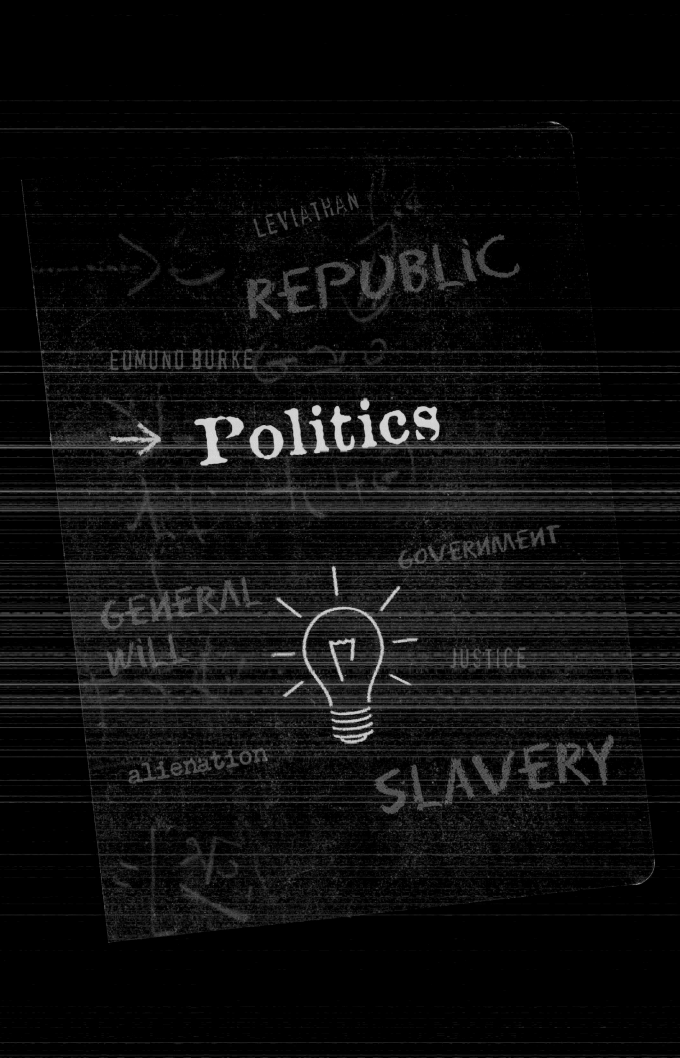

266 PLATO'S REPUBLIC

🎓 **PLATO'S REPUBLIC** puts forward the rather alarming thesis that the ideal society should be governed by benevolent philosopher-kings, who would rule with absolute power. This raises the specter of vicious authoritarianism, but Plato's contention is that as a result of their love of wisdom, access to the realm of perfect Forms, and lack of interest in the dirty business of personal advancement, philosopher-kings would govern strictly in the interests of a just society. It is his view that societies will only become virtuous when "those we now call kings and rulers really and truly become philosophers."

267 FAST FACT...

📖 **PLATO WROTE** *The Republic* in Athens in around 380 BC. The work is primarily concerned with defining and defending justice, but also makes bold forays into epistemology and metaphysics.

Plato's ideal society has a three-part structure. The philosopher-kings, or Guardians, embody the virtue of wisdom, and are charged with steering the ship of the state. At the next level down, soldiers, who embody the virtue of courage, must be prepared to defend the state against both external and internal enemies, with their lives if necessary. The rest of the people – producers, merchants and the like – are required to moderate their selfish desires in the interests of society as a whole.

According to Plato, a society organized along these lines will function harmoniously and exhibit justice at its heart.

We need philosophers!

268 FAST FACT...

📖 **PLATO'S REPUBLIC** was commented on and sometimes criticized by many later thinkers, including Aristotle, Zeno of Citium, Hegel and Popper.

269 ARISTOTLE ON SLAVERY

🎓 **ARISTOTLE** is a long way from being a bleeding-heart liberal when it comes to the issue of slavery, arguing that it *"is clear...that some men are by nature free, and others slaves, and that for these latter, slavery is both expedient and right."*

Aristotle outlines his ideas about slavery in Book 1 of *Politics*. His argument is rooted in the claim that nature has created a natural slave-type that is suited for a life of servitude and toil. This is a matter of both body and soul. The slave has a strong, well-endowed body that enables him to meet the demands of hard labor; but his soul is weak, and he is distinguished from a beast of burden only because he has the capacity to recognize the rational principle that governs his servitude. For Aristotle, then, slavery is right and legitimate, since it reflects the real differences that exist between human beings, an argument that does not sit well with modern thinkers.

It is worth noting that Aristotle's argument does not justify the enslavement of enemy soldiers. Victory on the battlefield, in and of itself, tells us nothing about the natural endowment of either the victors or the vanquished

270 FAST FACT...

📖 **SEVERAL** commentators have disputed the ordering of volumes in Aristotle's *Politics*, because of their apparently illogical flow.

271 SENECA ON SLAVERY

🎓 **THE ROMAN STOIC PHILOSOPHER**, Lucius Annaeus Seneca, rejected the idea that the minds of slaves were different from those of their masters.

"It is a mistake for anyone to believe that the condition of slavery penetrates into the whole being of a man.... Only the body is at the mercy and disposition of a master; but the mind is its own master. It is, therefore, the body that Fortune hands over to a master...that inner part cannot be delivered into bondage."

272 FAST FACT...

📖 **SENECA** was tutor to the Roman Emperor Nero, and was later forced to commit suicide due to his alleged involvement in a conspiracy to assassinate the emperor.

However, although Seneca argues that masters should treat their slaves with kindness and compassion, there is nothing to suggest that he thinks the institution of slavery itself is unjust. It is relevant here that he accepts the standard Stoic belief that nearly everybody is in a certain way enslaved. In his view, there is no strong distinction to be drawn between being a slave to certain desires or passions and being enslaved by a master.

273 FAST FACT...

📖 *"A gem cannot be polished without friction, nor a man perfected without trials."* – Seneca

274 FAST FACT...

📖 *"We are always complaining that our days are few, and acting as though there would be no end of them."* – Seneca

275 HOBBES'S LEVIATHAN

THOMAS HOBBES uses the term Leviathan to designate the absolute, sovereign authority, to which all individuals give up some of their rights in order to secure peace and security. In Hobbes's words, it is the "mortal god to which we owe, under the immortal God, our peace and defence." In concrete terms, he's talking about an absolute monarchy, perhaps in the style of Louis XIV of France.

The dangers of this conception are obvious. If there is no limit on the power of the Leviathan, then any abuse of power, even if it results in the vilest of tyrannies, just has to be accepted. In the light of the horrors of the twentieth century, this seems like a recipe for disaster; and even to Hobbes's contemporaries, the idea appeared a little cavalier. Thus, for example, John Locke asked despairingly why any person would be *"so foolish that they take care to avoid what mischiefs may be done them by polecats or foxes, but are content, nay think it safety, to be devoured by lions?"*

276 FAST FACT...

THE FAMOUS frontispiece of Hobbes's *Leviathan* features a giant crowned figure emerging from the landscape. His torso and arms are made up of over 300 human bodies.

The frontispiece of Hobbes's Leviathan

277 LOCKE'S TWO TREATISES OF GOVERNMENT

LIKE THOMAS HOBBES, John Locke uses the idea of a state of nature to ground his thoughts on political authority. However, Locke does not have as pessimistic a view as Hobbes about the fate of humanity in a state of nature, arguing that for the most part, our rational faculties will hold us back from doing harm to one another. Nevertheless, living without government is *"full of fears and continual dangers,"* so we are willing to sacrifice our executive power and resign it over to other people in order to ensure *"the mutual preservation of... lives, liberties and estates."*

Locke argues in favor of government based on the separation of powers. In particular, he stresses the merits of constitutional monarchy, where the monarch holds executive power and a parliamentary assembly holds legislative power. Crucially, it was his view that sovereignty ultimately belongs to the people, and that any government is obliged to govern in line with natural law and with the aim of preserving the lives and property of the general populace.

278 FAST FACT...

LOCKE was very unhappy with the early editions of *Two Treatises*, which were, apparently, replete with printers' errors.

279 FAST FACT...

LOCKE claimed *The Two Treatises'* purpose was to justify William III's ascension to the throne, yet the bulk of it was probably written nine years earlier.

280 FAST FACT...

LOCKE knew his work was politically dangerous and never acknowledged his authorship within his lifetime.

281 THE GENERAL WILL

🎓 **JEAN-JACQUES ROUSSEAU'S** concept of the general will was designed to address the question of how we can remain free, given that we are required to give up some of our freedom in order to secure the advantages of living peacefully with one another. His idea was that we can achieve a certain sort of freedom if our actions are directed by rules that we formulate ourselves when we come together as part of the sovereign body of a society.

This idea is notoriously slippery. In essence, the general will is an expression of the common good. However, it is not clear how this translates to real-world politics. At the very least, it requires that members of the sovereign body put aside their own personal interests and act only for the common good. As Rousseau put it, *"As long as several men assembled together consider themselves as a single body, they have only one will which is directed towards their common preservation and general well-being."*

282 FAST FACT...

📖 **THE FRENCH** edition of Locke's *Two Treatises*, read by Voltaire and Rousseau, did not even contain the First Treatise.

284 FAST FACT...

📖 *"But ... in what does this general will reside? Where can I consult it?... [The answer is:] In the principles of prescribed law of all civilized nations..."*
– Denis Diderot (1713–1784)

283 FAST FACT...

📖 **ROUSSEAU'S** concept of the general will has been criticized by many as amounting to a tyranny of the majority.

285 THE FRENCH REVOLUTION

THE FRENCH REVOLUTION is the name given to the period of political and social upheaval that swept through France from 1787–1799, which marked the end of the *ancien régime*, under which everybody had been a subject of the King of France. The Revolution would see the execution of King Louis XVI and his wife, Marie Antoinette, when the heads of state were quite literally removed by the guillotine.

The extent to which philosophical ideas contributed to the revolutionary movement is a matter of historical dispute. However, there is no doubt that the work of Enlightenment thinkers such as Montesquieu and Jean-Jacques Rousseau had the effect of undermining the traditions and old certainties that the Revolution set out to destroy.

The Revolution brought the issue of the foundations of legitimate political authority to the center stage, bringing an end to the notion that monarchs were appointed directly by God. The 1789 Declaration of the Rights of Man are steeped in Enlightenment philosophy and identify *"Liberty, Property, Safety and Resistance to Oppression"* as natural imprescriptible rights and hold that *"Men are born and remain free and equal in rights."*

286 THE RIGHTS OF MAN

ALTHOUGH THOMAS PAINE is not in the first rank of philosophers, he is notable for playing a part in the two great revolutionary moments of the eighteenth century: the American and French Revolutions.

His most famous work, *The Rights of Man*, is a defense of the principles of the French Revolution. At its center is the idea that human beings are born with equal, natural rights. However, because people live in societies, where they enjoy the advantages of cooperation, it is inevitable that sometimes their rights will be violated. Therefore, in order to safeguard all natural rights, people elect to transfer those rights they cannot uphold themselves – for example, the right to redress for a harm – into the protection of government.

Paine argues that government gains its rightful authority from the people as a whole. Legitimate government is necessarily of the people and for the people. In fact, it was Paine's belief that only democratic republicanism is properly legitimate, because it best represents the collective rights that people are unable to defend individually.

287 FAST FACT...

PAINE'S *Rights of Man* is a defense of the French Revolution against Edmund Burke's attack in *Reflections on the Revolution in France* (1790).

288 FAST FACT...

RIGHTS OF MAN sparked public outrage in England. Paine fled to France, but was tried in absentia and convicted for seditious libel.

LEFT: Ferdinand Delacroix (1798-1863) "Liberty Leading the People" (1830).

THE DECLARATION OF THE RIGHTS OF MAN AND THE CITIZEN
(LA DÉCLARATION DES DROITS DE L'HOMME ET DU CITOYEN), 1789

1 Men are born and remain free and equal in rights. Social distinctions may be based only on considerations of the common good.

2 The aim of every political association is the preservation of the natural and imprescriptible rights of man. These rights are Liberty, Property, Safety and Resistance to Oppression.

3 The source of all sovereignty lies essentially in the Nation. No corporate body, no individual may exercise any authority that does not expressly emanate from it.

4 Liberty consists in being able to do anything that does not harm others: thus, the exercise of the natural rights of every man has no bounds other than those that ensure to the other members of society the enjoyment of these same rights. These bounds may be determined only by Law.

5 The Law has the right to forbid only those actions that are injurious to society. Nothing that is not forbidden by Law may be hindered, and no one may be compelled to do what the Law does not ordain.

6 The Law is the expression of the general will. All citizens have the right to take part, personally or through their representatives, in its making. It must be the same for all, whether it protects or punishes. All citizens, being equal in its eyes, shall be equally eligible to all high offices, public positions and employments, according to their ability, and without other distinction than that of their virtues and talents.

7 No man may be accused, arrested or detained except in the cases determined by the Law, and following the procedure that it has prescribed. Those who solicit, expedite, carry out, or cause to be carried out arbitrary orders must be punished; but any citizen summoned or apprehended by virtue of the Law, must give instant obedience; resistance makes him guilty.

8 The Law must prescribe only the punishments that are strictly and evidently necessary; and no one may be punished except by virtue of a Law drawn up and promulgated before the offense is committed, and legally applied.

9 As every man is presumed innocent until he has been declared guilty, if it should be considered necessary to arrest him, any undue harshness that is not required to secure his person must be severely curbed by Law.

10 No one may be disturbed on account of his opinions, even religious ones, as long as the manifestation of such opinions does not interfere with the established Law and Order.

11 The free communication of ideas and of opinions is one of the most precious rights of man. Any citizen may therefore speak, write and publish freely, except what is tantamount to the abuse of this liberty in the cases determined by Law.

12 To guarantee the Rights of Man and of the Citizen a public force is necessary; this force is therefore established for the benefit of all, and not for the particular use of those to whom it is entrusted.

13 For the maintenance of the public force, and for administrative expenses, a general tax is indispensable; it must be equally distributed among all citizens, in proportion to their ability to pay.

14 All citizens have the right to ascertain, by themselves, or through their representatives, the need for a public tax, to consent to it freely, to watch over its use, and to determine its proportion, basis, collection and duration.

15 Society has the right to ask a public official for an accounting of his administration.

16 Any society in which no provision is made for guaranteeing rights or for the separation of powers, has no Constitution.

17 Since the right to Property is inviolable and sacred, no one may be deprived thereof, unless public necessity, legally ascertained, obviously requires it, and just and prior indemnity has been paid.

289 THE FIRST FEMINIST

THE EIGHTEENTH-CENTURY radical, Mary Wollstonecraft, was a champion of the rights of women at a time when women were not even on the radar of most Enlightenment thinkers. She argues that women's inequality is woven into the fabric of the social system. Women are brought up in a manner that destroys their intellectual and rational abilities; they learn that they are subservient to men; and are encouraged to cultivate a docile sexuality that is designed to be appealing to men.

It was Wollstonecraft's view that things would only change if women's education was radically restructured. Specifically, women, just as men, had to be taught to develop their rational capabilities. The best kind of education *"is such an exercise of the understanding as is best calculated to strengthen the body and form the heart. Or, in other words, to enable the individual to attain such habits of virtue as will render it independent."*

290 FAST FACT...

📖 *"Till women are more rationally educated, the progress in human virtue and improvement in knowledge must receive continual checks."* – Mary Wollstonecraft (1759–1797)

291 FAST FACT...

📖 **MARY WOLLSTONECRAFT** was the mother of Mary Shelley, the author of *Frankenstein*.

The Suffragette movement campaigned for women's rights, particularly the right to vote in political elections.

EXTRACTS FROM A VINDICATION OF THE RIGHTS OF WOMAN (1792)

"Women are told from their infancy, and taught by the example of their mothers, that a little knowledge of human weakness, justly termed cunning, softness of temper, outward obedience, and a scrupulous attention to a puerile kind of propriety, will obtain for them the protection of man; and should they be beautiful, everything else is needless, for at least twenty years of their lives."

"Strengthen the female mind by enlarging it, and there will be an end to blind obedience; but as blind obedience is ever sought for by power, tyrants and sensualists are in the right endeavor to keep woman in the dark, because only want slaves, and the latter a plaything."

"I lament that women are systematically degraded by receiving the trivial attentions which men think it manly to pay to the sex, when in fact, they are insultingly supporting their own superiority. It is not condescension to bow to an inferior. So ludicrous, in fact, do these ceremonies appear to me that I scarcely am able to govern my muscles when I see a man with eager and serious solicitude to lift a handkerchief or shut a door, when the lady could have done it herself, had she only moved a pace or two."

"Women ought to have representatives, instead of being arbitrarily governed without any direct share allowed them in the deliberations of government."

292 EDMUND BURKE'S CONSERVATISM

EDMUND BURKE is today acclaimed as one of the originators of modern political conservatism. In particular, his defense of the virtues of tradition and prejudice in *Reflections on the Revolution in France* is considered exemplary as a statement of conservative principles.

Burke's central thesis was that it is a catastrophic error to suppose that the past can be simply wiped away and a new society constructed upon a set of abstract principles. The leaders of the French Revolution showed no awareness of the importance of tradition, custom and sentiment, which meant the whole movement was bound to end in bloody failure.

Burke argues that it is just too risky to allow ideas about natural rights to trump an established system of government. Moreover, the shared traditions, beliefs and habits of a nation, instantiated and passed on through extant institutions, function to secure the benefits that have been hard-won by previous generations.

293 FAST FACT...

DESPITE his reputation as the founder of modern conservatism, Burke supported the American Revolution and, initially, the French Revolution.

Although conservative thought is not fashionable in most philosophical circles nowadays, it is to Burke's tremendous credit that he got it pretty much right about the French Revolution. The Jacobin Terror occurred exactly as he predicted it would.

I told you so!

294 FAST FACT...

"But what is liberty without wisdom, and without virtue? It is the greatest of all possible evils; for it is folly, vice, and madness, without tuition or restraint." – Edmund Burke (1729–1797)

295 MARX ON ALIENATION

IN MANY WAYS, Karl Marx's ideas about alienation constitute the moral underpinning of his revolutionary politics. If we ask why we should look forward to the overthrow of capitalism, the answer is that it marks the beginning of the end of our alienation.

Marx's concept of alienation is tied up with ideas he had about the fundamental nature of human beings. Simply put, Marx thought that it is in our nature to cooperate with each other in freely chosen labor. It is in this way that we come to a proper understanding of ourselves, and of our relationships with each other and the world of objects.

296 FAST FACT...

📖 Marx's favorite maxim was *"Nihil humani a me alienum puto"* (Nothing human is alien to me).

However, the problem is that in class societies we have no control over the labor process, which means we are alienated from our essential nature. Marx describes the alienation of the proletarian as follows: *"...he does not fulfil himself in his work but denies himself, has a feeling of misery rather than well-being, does not develop freely his mental and physical energies but is physically exhausted and mentally debased."*

297 ENGELS ON THE FAMILY

IT IS THE STANDARD MARXIST LINE that the abolition of class distinctions will bring about a society without systematic inequality or conflict. However, it is not at all clear why this should be the case. Take the position of women in society, for example. It is far from obvious why collective ownership of the means of production will bring an end to sexual inequality.

Friedrich Engels attempts to answer this question in *The Origin of the Family, Private Property and the State*. He argues that women are oppressed because they are confined within the domestic sphere, a situation which exists in order to ensure that there are clear lines of descent so men can pass on property to their rightful heirs.

This means that if private property is abolished, then there is no longer any need for women to be confined within the home, which removes the material basis of their oppression. As Engels puts it, *"The supremacy of the man in marriage is the simple consequence of his economic supremacy, and with the abolition of the latter will disappear of itself."*

A statue of Marx and Engels in Alexanderplatz, Berlin

298 PROUDHON'S ANARCHISM

🎓 **PIERRE-JOSEPH PROUDHON**, a nineteenth-century French social theorist, is famous for declaring that all property is theft, and for his willingness to describe himself as an anarchist. By this he did not mean that he was committed to the destruction of the social order, but rather that he favored mutual self-regulation, and order without government or sovereign authority.

Proudhon's anarchism was partly motivated by a deep mistrust of all forms of authority. This put him on a collision course with socialist and communist strands of left-wing thought. His anti-authoritarianism is perfectly illustrated in a plea for tolerance he made to Karl Marx:

> "...let us not, merely because we are at the head of a movement, make ourselves the leaders of a new intolerance, let us not pose as the apostles of a new religion, even if it be the religion of logic, the religion of reason. Let us gather together and encourage all protests...let us never regard a question as exhausted, and when we have used our last argument, let us begin again."

Pierre-Joseph Proudhon

299 FAST FACT...

📖 **PROUDHON** was the first person to call himself an anarchist.

300 FAST FACT...

📖 "[Laws] are spider webs for the rich and mighty, steel chains for the poor and weak, fishing nets in the hands of government." – Pierre-Joseph Proudhon (1809–1865)

301 F. A. HAYEK – THE MODERN LIBERAL

🎓 **THE HORRORS** of National Socialism and Stalinism had a profound effect on the worldview of twentieth-century economist, F. A. Hayek. His renowned advocacy of small government was rooted in a belief that a large state brings the threat of totalitarianism. He did not think that it is possible to plan centrally while at the same time preserve individual liberty. Attempts to control societies and economies, which are *"spontaneous orders,"* inevitably result in a move towards authoritarianism.

According to Hayek, governments should be concerned merely with ensuring that the conditions exist for people to pursue their own aims without interference. In effect, what this means is that governments should do no more than enforce the rule of law. Certainly, there should be no attempt to manipulate the market in order to secure outcomes that are considered more equitable or fair. Thus, for example, Hayek opposed systems of progressive taxation, where the rich pay a higher proportion of their income in tax than the poor, on the grounds that they violate the principle that everybody is equal before the law.

302 FAST FACT...

📖 *"Personally I prefer a liberal dictator to democratic government lacking liberalism."* – Friedrich August von Hayek (1899–1992)

303 FAST FACT...

📖 **HAYEK** was second cousin to Ludwig Wittgenstein. As officers during World War I, the two of them discussed philosophy.

304 LIBERTARIANISM

LIBERTARIANISM is an individualist social and political philosophy that denies that the state has a role to play in the private conduct of individuals. The extent to which libertarians see a role at all for the state varies. Anarcho-libertarians, for example, believe that the abolition of the state is a prerequisite for a free society, whereas libertarians more inclined towards a minimal state position see a role for government in protecting people from aggression, theft, and the like.

The view that the state has no right meddling in the private affairs of its citizens is a form of social liberalism. In concrete terms, it is associated with a constellation of beliefs, for example the notion that sexual behavior, gun ownership and drug use should not be subject to government regulation.

Social liberalism is often allied with a fiscal conservatism. Most libertarians, certainly in North America, deny that government has any role to play in attempting to secure greater social justice or equality via the taxation system.

Peace and love, man

305 FAST FACT

EMILE ARMAND (1872–1963) was an influential individualist anarchist in the early twentieth century, advocating free love, communal living and pacifism.

306 FEMINISM

FEMINISM is not any one thing. It is simultaneously an approach to understanding the world and a social movement; it has radical and less radical variants; and it is said to have had different waves. At its most general, feminism is a set of ideas that advocates for women's rights, focusing in particular on the way in which structured inequality negatively impacts on the life chances of women. However, there are large differences between feminists in terms of how they view sexual inequality and what they think ought to be done about it.

Emmeline and Christabel Pankhurst, leaders of the Women's Social and Political Union (1857-1928)

A liberal feminist approach will tend to focus on issues of political and legal equality. Thus, for example, Betty Friedan, author of *The Feminine Mystique* – a seminal text of second wave feminism – was heavily involved in the campaign in the United States for equality in the workplace.

However, more radical approaches reject the idea that equality of opportunity will be enough to secure female emancipation. If society is thoroughly patriarchal, then the position of women will not be improved until gender relations are radically restructured.

307 FAST FACT...

📖 **THE FIRST WAVE** of feminism focused on gaining women's suffrage. Early leaders included Elizabeth Cady Stanton and Emmeline Pankhurst.

308 KATE MILLET'S SEXUAL POLITICS

🎓 **IN HER GROUNDBREAKING WORK**, *Sexual Politics*, Kate Millet argues that gender is almost entirely socially constructed. The differences between the sexes in terms of temperament, preferences, interests and behavior are a function of different patterns of socialization. According to Millet, this applies even to sexual preferences, which are so much the product of learning that *"even the act of coitus itself is the product of a long series of learned responses – responses to the patterns and attitudes, even as to the object of sexual choice, which are set up for us by our social environment."*

309 FAST FACT...

📖 **KATE MILLET** was an unknown, impoverished, New York sculptor when Sexual Politics was published. It was based on her doctoral thesis.

It is Millet's view that human personalities are molded by structures of patriarchy that promote stereotypical gender identities. Women are socialized to be passive, docile and ineffectual, whereas men learn to be aggressive, intelligent and effective. Millet claims that in their primary childbearing and child-rearing roles, there is little to separate women from animals.

310 FAST FACT...

📖 *"Her condescending, destructive, bitterly anti-male method of approaching art was adopted as dogma*

Millet's ideas have attracted criticism from her feminist colleagues for their tendency to infantilize women, but she remains an important figure in feminist thought.

The toys we are given as children could be seen as an example of gender being assigned through socialization.

311 FEMINISM AND PORNOGRAPHY

THERE IS NO CONSENSUS VIEW amongst feminists about the issue of pornography. Radical feminists, such as Catherine MacKinnon and Andrea Dworkin, have been at the forefront of campaigns to get at least certain forms of pornography prohibited. However, sex-positive feminists, such as Gayle Rubin, have argued that these kinds of campaigns tend to stray dangerously close to the territory occupied by anti-feminist conservatives.

MacKinnon and Dworkin define pornography as *"the graphic sexually explicit subordination of women through pictures and words."* So, for example, images of women enjoying servility and humiliation would count as pornography under this definition. In this sense, pornography mirrors the patriarchal structure of society and functions to reproduce women's subordination.

However, there are many difficulties associated with this analysis. Not least, it is not clear how one would decide whether particular images and words count as pornographic. Moreover, focusing merely on the misogynistic aspects of pornography is to ignore the benefits that it can bring to women in terms of widening their sexual horizons, challenging traditional conceptions of femininity, and so on.

312 SPECIESISM

THERE IS LITTLE DOUBT that most of us routinely discriminate in favor of our own species at the expense of other species. For example, the majority of people in the West eat meat. But consider also that even amongst vegetarians, the number of people who would choose to rescue a dog rather than a new born child from a fire is vanishingly small. In his book, *Animal Liberation*, Peter Singer asks how we might justify this sort of discrimination.

The most obvious justification will point to the higher mental faculties that human beings possess. However, this line of thought quickly runs into a number of rather difficult problems. For example, it seems to require that if we have to decide between saving the life of a coma patient or that of a great ape, we should choose the great ape.

Singer argues that favoring humans over another species just because we belong to the same species is "speciesism," a form of prejudice just like any other. There may be occasions when it is perfectly legitimate to discriminate in favor of human beings, but we have to have reasons for doing so other than the mere fact that we belong to the same species.

313 FAST FACT...

"The central analogy to the civil rights movement and the women's movement is trivializing and ahistorical." – Peter Staudenmaier, criticizing speciesism

314 ENVIRONMENTAL ETHICS

🎓 **THE DISCIPLINE** of environmental ethics, which emerged in the 1970s, aims to extend the domain of moral philosophy into the non-human world. It tends to ask questions about the moral status of human interaction with the environment, and also about the value of the environment in and of itself. Here are some of the questions that are dealt with under environmental ethics:

- Is the destruction of the environment intrinsically wrong or is it wrong because it damages future human beings?

- Is it permissible to build dams at great expense to the environment if the result is a plentiful supply of drinking water for an *"at risk"* population?

- Is deliberately manipulating the genetic makeup of an entire species ever justified (consider the case of malaria-bearing mosquitoes, for example)?

Perhaps the most contentious issue in the field of environmental ethics is the question of whether the environment has intrinsic value that does not depend upon the existence of sentient beings. This question is perhaps most likely to be answered in the affirmative by advocates of what is known as *"deep ecology."*

315 FAST FACT...

📖 **THE ROOTS** of environmental ethics can be traced to Aldo Leopold's 1949 essay, "A Sand County Almanac," and Rachel Carson's 1962 book *Silent Spring*.

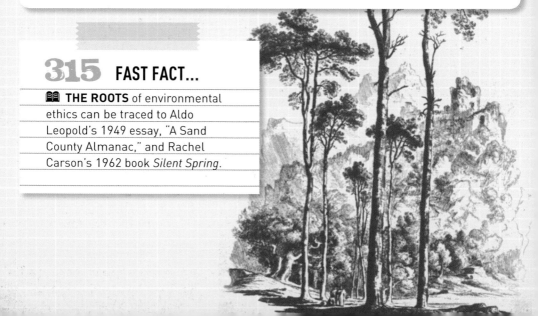

316 DISTRIBUTIVE JUSTICE

🎓 **EVERY SOCIETY** needs some way of dividing up the spoils of economic activity. The principles that guide this process are known as principles of distributive justice.

Consider, for example, a strict egalitarian principle, which requires that the material goods of a society are shared equally between every citizen. It is easy to see how this principle will run into difficulties. Take the issue of reward, for example. The possibility that a person could work two jobs and be no more rewarded than a person who chooses not to work at all seems obviously unjust.

Perhaps, then, a principle that emphasizes equality of opportunity would work better. Again problems quickly emerge. For example, equality of opportunity will tend to reward those who, through no merit of their own, are endowed with greater talents. Again, it does not seem fair that a person could end up badly off just because they happen to have been born with less than average intelligence, for instance.

These sorts of complexities are indicative of the difficulty with developing defensible theories of distributive justice. Unsurprisingly, there is no general agreement among philosophers about how society should allocate its material (and other) goods.

501

compatibilism

LAPLACE'S DEMON

FISSION PROBLEM

OTHER MINDS

PANPSYCHISM

mind-body problem

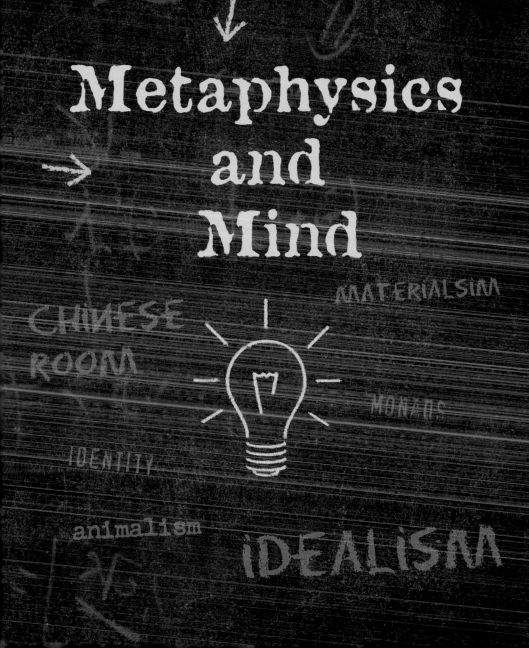

Metaphysics and Mind

ATOMISM

MATERIALSIM

CHINESE
ROOM

MONADS

IDENTITY

animalism

IDEALISM

319 ATOMISM

ACCORDING TO the atomist philosophers of Ancient Greece, Leucippus and Democritus, the world is made up of two sorts of things: atoms and void.

The atoms are indivisible, solid and vary in shape and size. They are infinite in number and constantly move around within the similarly infinite void. The everyday objects of the material world come into existence as a result of the collisions that occur between atoms:

...overtaking each other they collide, and some are shaken away in any chance direction, while others, becoming intertwined one with another according to the congruity of their shapes, sizes, positions and arrangements, stay together and so effect the coming into being of compound bodies.

The fundamental stuff of reality, therefore, is unchanging and eternal, but it combines together to form the manifold and changing objects of our experience.

The similarity between the atomist worldview and modern scientific ideas about atoms is striking. However, it would be incorrect to think of the atomists as proto-scientists, since their ideas were rooted in metaphysical speculation rather than empirical research.

320 FAST FACT...

PLATO is said to have disliked Democritus, father of atomism, so much that he wanted all of his books to be burned.

321 MATERIALISM

ATOMISM IS thoroughly materialist in character. It holds that the building blocks of reality are material things and nothing else. In this sense, materialism is an ontological position, which asserts that everything that is real is material (rather than, for example, mind or spirit). This claim normally comes down to the proposition that it has only physical properties, such as a location in space and time, size, shape, and so on.

Although we are familiar with thinking of reality in material terms, the difficulty with claiming that everything that is real is material is clear. What about psychological states, for example? There are different ways of handling this question from within a materialist framework, the most radical of which is probably a position termed *"eliminative materialism."* This holds that mental phenomena, such as beliefs and desires, just do not exist. If we are convinced that they do exist, it means only that we remain committed to the remnants of a folk psychology that will come to be supplanted by modern neuroscience.

322 FAST FACT...

📖 **THE PHILOSOPHICAL** concept of materialism developed independently in Europe, India and China between 800 and 200 BC.

323 LEIBNIZ'S MONADS

🎓 **LIKE THE ATOMISTS**, Gottfried Leibniz believed that reality was built out of an infinite number of simple, non-divisible, entities.

> The Monad...is nothing but a simple substance, which enters into compounds. By "simple" is meant "without parts."... These Monads are the real atoms of nature and, in a word, the elements of things.

However, Leibniz's monads are a very different sort of thing to the atoms of the atomists. For a start, they lack extension, spatial position, shape, or any other physical attributes. They are also entirely independent of each other, only appearing to interact, which means they must be the source of their own activity. Perhaps most disconcertingly, Leibniz claims that monads are endowed with perception, which allows each of them to follow an individual set of rules that, when combined. generate the universe's preordained harmony.

Leibniz argued that the monads constitute an infinite hierarchy. God, the supreme monad, is at the apex; human beings, as a result of their capacity for self-awareness and rational thought, come near the top; bare monads, only marginally percipient, are positioned at the bottom.

324 FAST FACT...

📖 **LEIBNIZ** wrote *Monadology* in his late 60s, during a stay in Vienna (1712–14). He died in 1716.

325 FAST FACT...

📖 *"And as every present state of a simple substance is naturally a consequence of its preceding state, so its present is pregnant with its future."* – Gottfried Leibniz (1646–1716)

326 FAST FACT...

📖 **THE LATEST** research suggests that the majority of the universe is composed of Dark Matter and Dark Energy, contradicting historical materialism, which states that "traditional matter" is all that exists.

327 PANPSYCHISM

LEIBNIZ'S DOCTRINE of monads is a form of panpsychism in that it suggests the fundamental building blocks of reality are perceptually aware; that is, they possess mentality. The British philosopher, Timothy Sprigge, has defined panpsychism as follows:

> "I hold that panpsychism is true, namely, that the inner being or inherent nature of the physical world is "mental" in the sense that it consists in streams of consciousness, feeling or experience, interacting with each other in a law-like way and that science charts the abstract structure of the system they form, and of which the world of everyday life is a pictorial appearance."

To the modern mind, the idea that physical things are mental on the inside is difficult to believe. However, though panpsychism is a somewhat scandalous view within philosophical circles, this does not mean that there is nothing to recommend it. In particular, panpsychism has a ready explanation for the existence of mind – or consciousness – in the world, something which so far has almost entirely eluded physicalist approaches to the question.

328 FAST FACT...

ANAXAGORAS, an early idealist thinker, was known as Nous (Mind) because he taught that all things were created by Mind.

329 FAST FACT...

"The Universe begins to look more like a great thought than like a great machine" – 20th century British scientist, Sir James Jeans

330 FAST FACT...

PANPSYCHISM is derived from *pan*, meaning "everywhere" and *psyche*, meaning "mind."

331 IDEALISM

PHILOSOPHICAL *"idealism"* is best understood in contrast with the idea of materialism. While materialism asserts that everything that exists is material, idealism asserts that the most basic reality is in some sense mental. Panpsychism, then, can be seen as a form of idealism.

Unfortunately, philosophers do not use term *idealism* in a consistent way, which means that a number of different approaches have attracted the label. For example, Berkeley's idea that physical objects are no more than collections of sense impressions is sometimes called *"subjective idealism"* and Kant's metaphysics, which sees the mind as actively constituting the world of experience, tends to be referred to as *"transcendental idealism."*

Timothy Sprigge has noted that it is possible to distinguish between the various idealisms in terms of whether their claims are *ontological* or *epistemological*. This is not as complicated as it sounds. Ontological idealism is the view that it is definitely true that reality is mind-dependent, and common sense notions that assert otherwise are wrong. Epistemological idealism asserts only that the most plausible view of the physical world, including the claim that it is mind independent, is true only for us.

332 LIBET'S NEUROLOGICAL CHALLENGE

IN A SERIES of experiments conducted in the 1980s, Benjamin Libet showed that freely chosen acts are initiated unconsciously in the brain even before a person consciously knows that they are going to act.

The inspiration for these experiments was the discovery that conscious acts are preceded by the build up of an electrical charge in the brain. Libet devised an experiment to test whether this *"readiness potential,"* as it is called, occurs before a person knows that they are going to act. He wired participants up to an EEG machine, and asked them to perform a simple task. They were also asked to record a clock-time associated with their first awareness that they were going to act. This gave Libet three bits of data: the time of the act, the time of the person's awareness that they were going to act, and the time of the appearance of the readiness potential.

The experiment showed that the readiness potential occurred in the brain some 350 milliseconds before a person knew that they were going to act. This led Libet to the startling conclusion that the *"initiation of the freely voluntary act appears to begin in the brain unconsciously."* If this is right, it seems to threaten the idea that we have free choice.

333 LAPLACE'S DEMON

🎓 **THE NINETEENTH-CENTURY** French physicist, Pierre-Simon Laplace, is notable for the following quotation, which sets out the argument now known as *"Laplace's Demon.*

"We may regard the present state of the universe as the effect of its past and the cause of its future. An intellect which at any given moment knew all of the forces that animate nature and the mutual positions of the beings that compose it, if this intellect were vast enough to submit the data to analysis, could condense into a single formula the movement of the greatest bodies of the universe and that of the lightest atom; for such an intellect nothing could be uncertain and the future just like the past would be present before its eyes."

The idea being articulated here is known as causal determinism. It holds that every event is merely an effect of past events. The philosophical significance of this idea lies mainly in its implications for free will. If the future is simply an effect of the present, which in turn is an effect of the past, then it doesn't seem to leave any room for free choice: we were always going to make the choices that we make.

334 FAST FACT...

📖 *"We may regard the present state of the universe as the effect of its past and the cause of its future."* – Pierre-Simon Laplace (1749–1827)

335 FAST FACT...

📖 **PIERRE-SIMON LAPLACE** was one of the first scientists to suggest the possibility of black holes and gravitational collapse.

336 FAST FACT...

📖 *"Life's most important questions are, for the most part, nothing but probability problems."* – Pierre-Simon Laplace

337 THE MIND-BODY PROBLEM

RENÉ DESCARTES set out the mind-body problem in his *Meditations*. Put simply, the problem is that the mind seems to be one sort of thing and the material world another sort of thing, which means it is not clear how they interact with each other.

According to Descartes, the essence of mind is thought, which is *unextended*; whereas the essence of matter (or the body) is *extension*, and extended things cannot think.

The problem with this conception is immediately obvious. It seems indisputable that the mind affects the body (and vice versa). If I decide to have a drink, for example, then I have no difficulty willing my arm to pick up a glass. However, if mind and body are different sorts of things, it is not clear how they can work together like this.

338 FAST FACT...

DESCARTES did not believe that animals had a soul, which led him to conclude that they could not feel pain. His practice of vivisection was widely followed in Europe at the time.

339 FAST FACT...

DESCARTES chose the pineal gland in the brain as the seat of the soul because, unlike other brain parts, it appeared to be unitary (in fact, it has two hemispheres).

Descartes did not have an adequate response to this problem. He suggested that the pineal gland was the location at which mind and body interact, but nobody was convinced. Even in the present day, we are not really any closer to working out the precise relationship between mind and brain.

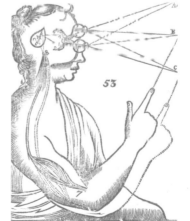

An illustration showing the pineal gland and its supposed connection with the mind-body problem

340 INCOMPATIBILISM

THERE IS NO general agreement among philosophers about the implications of causal determinism for free will. Incompatibilist philosophers, such as Immanuel Kant, define free will in such a way so as to make it logically incompatible with the truth of determinism. According to incompatibilists, a choice or act is only free if it is not an effect – or, to express this in technical terms, if it is *originated* – yet remains under the control of the acting agent. Therefore, it follows that if determinism is true, then there is no such thing as free choice (because determinism asserts that all our choices are effects).

To get a sense of the impulse that lies behind the incompatibilist position, consider the issue of moral responsibility. If we cannot act in any way other than we do act, do we possess the sort of freedom that would make us morally responsible for our actions? How can we be culpable for a choice that we were destined to make from the moment we were born?

Are our future actions already mapped out from the moment we are born?

341 FAST FACT...

ROBERT KANE, a leading incompatibilist philosopher, believes in the existence of alternative actions and that we have ultimate responsibility over our choices.

342 COMPATIBILISM

COMPATIBILIST PHILOSOPHERS, such as David Hume, take a different view. They argue that a free action is one that flows from the desires, intentions and dispositions of the acting agent. If a person is not suffering from a mental illness, does not have a gun held to their head, or is not in some other way compelled to act, then they are making free choices. In this sense, free will is logically compatible with the truth of determinism.

343 FAST FACT...

ROMAN PHILOSOPHER
Lucretius (99–55 BC) asserted that the free will arises out of the random, chaotic movements of atoms, called *clinamen*.

344 FAST FACT...

"Man can do what he wills but he cannot will what he wills"
– Arthur Schopenhauer (1788–1860)

According to the compatibilist view, the fact that a person is always going to act in a certain way does not make it any less *their* act. Determinism does not assert that no actions flow from an agent, it just says that these actions have a causal background. The fact that a person is in some sense the product of a vastly complex network of causal relations does not make them any less of a person. Free acts, whatever their causal background, are just those that flow from an individual's intentions and desires.

As long as we are not being threatened or suffering from a mental illness, the choices we make are free choices.

345 ELIMINATIVE MATERIALISM

🎓 **ELIMINATIVE MATERIALISM** is the rather disconcerting view that our normal psychological language, or folk psychology, which posits mental states such as beliefs, desires, hopes, the will, and so on, is deeply flawed, and that it will turn out that many, if not all, of these states do not exist.

Part of the motivation for this idea is the the data we have from neuroscience; it tells us that there is nothing in the head apart from the physical brain. In other words, there is no non-physical mind, or soul, of the kind that might survive the destruction of the brain; and we think, feel, make decisions and plan as a result of processes going on in the brain.

If this is right, then it is possible that just as phlogiston (a fire-like element first invoked in the seventeenth century to explain combustion) did not correspond to anything that actually exists, neither do the mental states put forward by folk psychology.

346 FAST FACT...

📖 **ELIMINATIVIST PHILOSOPHER,** Paul Churchland suggests that consciousness might be a type of neural network with its hub located in part of the thalamus, in the brain.

Is everything we think, fear and believe merely a result of brain functions?

347 THE TURING TEST

🎓 **THE QUESTION** of how to determine whether a machine is conscious and intelligent, rather than merely exhibiting the characteristics of these attributes, will become increasingly pressing as technological improvements bring advances in the field of artificial intelligence (AI).

The most famous approach to this question is the Turing Test, devised by the computer scientist, Alan Turing. In essence, the Turing Test asks whether or not a computer can pass itself off as a human during a conversation. If it can, then we are justified in concluding that the machine at least thinks. Turing argued that the test can be extended in order to answer the more specific question of whether a machine is conscious. It would be possible to devise an interrogation that could only be completed successfully by machines that have access to the sorts of insights that only conscious beings are able to draw upon (e.g. environmental, historical, moral).

348 FAST FACT...

📖 **IN 1966**, ELIZA, a computer program created by Joseph Weizenbaum, controversially "passed" the Turing Test by fooling some people into believing that she was a real person.

349 FAST FACT...

📖 *"I believe that at the end of the [20th] century ... one will be able to speak of machines thinking without expecting to be contradicted."*
– Alan Turing (1912–1954)

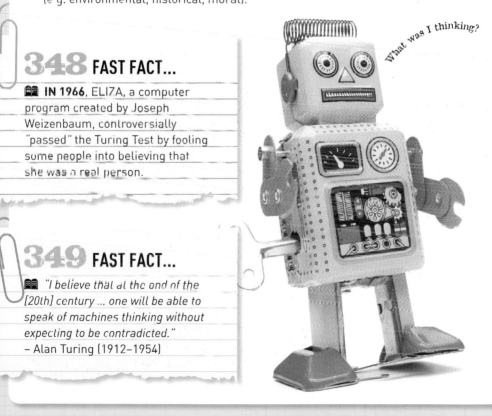

What was I thinking?

350 SEARLE'S CHINESE ROOM

🎓 **JOHN SEARLE** asks us to imagine a scenario that has the following form. You are locked in a room, and sets of Chinese symbols are delivered to you. You neither speak nor understand Chinese, but you have access to a set of formal rules for manipulating the symbols of the language. For every set of symbols that arrives, you apply the rules, and then write down, on a piece of paper, a specific combination of symbols in response, which you pass out of the room.

By applying the rules in this manner, you are producing perfectly understandable Chinese. It does not mean anything to you, of course, since you have no idea what the symbols mean – you proceed merely by recognizing their various shapes. However, if a Chinese speaker was outside passing in Chinese symbols, then they would understand your responses.

This raises the possibility that a *"Chinese Room"* would pass the Turing Test. In other words, a Chinese speaker would not be able to tell the difference between talking to the room and talking to a native Chinese speaker. However, this seems to make the Turing Test redundant, because its whole point is to determine whether there is any thinking going on, and we know that there is no thinking or understanding in the Chinese room, just the automatic manipulation of symbols.

Searle's thought experiment first appeared in his 1980 paper "Minds, Brains, and Programs." It has been described as *"an exemplar of philosophical clarity and purity."*

351 FAST FACT...

📖 "The Chinese Room" was originally offered in response to suggestions that machines can think, but it has come to be viewed as an important contribution to the philosophy of the mind.

352 CHINESE ROOM – THE SYSTEM REPLY

🎓 **SEARLE'S CHINESE ROOM** thought experiment has generated a huge amount of literature and a lot of controversy. Its intention was to demonstrate that a machine following a computational algorithm might be able to simulate the ability to think, but it could never actually think. However, by not everybody is convinced that it has demonstrated this.

353 FAST FACT...

📖 **NED BLOCK** has been a judge at the Loebner Prize contest, an annual contest in the tradition of the Turing Test.

354 FAST FACT...

📖 **NED BLOCK** argues that the China Brain would function like a human being, but would not be conscious. It would be what is known as a "philosophical zombie."

Perhaps the most common objection to Searle's argument is what is called *"the system reply."* This holds that though it is true that the person inside the room does not understand Chinese, the whole system – which includes the person, the rules, the paper, and so on – does understand Chinese. In this sense, the person is equivalent to the CPU of a computer: they are responsible for implementing the rules of symbol manipulation, but they are not the locus of the system's understanding. If this objection is correct, it means that Searle is looking in the wrong place for understanding (and thought): it is the Chinese room itself that understands Chinese, not the person in the room.

355 WHAT DOES MARY KNOW?

🎓 **MARY IS A BRILLIANT SCIENTIST** who knows literally everything there is to know about the neurophysiology of color vision. However, somewhat ironically, she has never actually seen a color herself, since she has spent her entire life inside a black and white room.

356 FAST FACT...

📖 **FRANK JACKSON'S** father, Allan Cameron Jackson, also a philosopher, was a student of Ludwig Wittgenstein

This situation prompts an interesting question: will Mary learn something new about the world when she actually experiences seeing color for the first time?

357 FAST FACT...

📖 **FRANK JACKSON** delivered the John Locke lectures at Oxford University in 1995, as his father had done in 1957–8, making them the first father–son pair to do so.

According to Frank Jackson, who devised this thought experiment, it is obvious that she will. This means that while she is inside the black and white room, her knowledge of color is incomplete, despite the fact she knows everything there is to know about the physiology of color vision (in other words, despite the fact she has complete *physical knowledge* of color and how it is perceived). It follows, therefore, that the claim that there are only physical facts and that knowledge is necessarily knowledge of physical things is false. Specifically, it leaves out the knowledge we gain from *qualia*, the raw feelings that are part and parcel of being conscious.

358 FAST FACT...

📖 **THE** "Mary's Room" thought experiment is a major theme of David Lodge's 2001 novel *Thinks....* Frank Jackson makes an appearance in the novel.

359 FAST FACT...

📖 **JACKSON** proposed the thought experiment to support the knowledge argument against physicalism. However, he later rejected this argument and now supports the physicalist viewpoint.

360 EPIPHENOMENALISM

🎓 **EPIPHENOMENALISM** is the view that mental events (for example, a decision to act) are caused by physical events – in particular, by neural events in the brain – but have no causal effect themselves upon the physical world. So while it might seem as if the experience of pain makes us yelp, or fear causes us to tremble, in reality these sorts of physical occurrences (yelping and trembling) are actually the effect of a network of underlying physical (neurological) causes.

> "The consciousness of brutes would appear to be related to the mechanism of their body simply as a collateral product of its working, and to be as completely without any power of modifying that working as the steam-whistle which accompanies the work of a locomotive engine is without influence on its machinery."

The major thing to be said in favor of epiphenomenalism is that it does not try to claim that mental stuff is identical to physical stuff, but at the same time it does not require us to think that anything other than physical events can affect the physical world.

361 FAST FACT...

📖 **AMERICAN PHILOSOPHER**
Jerry Fodor coined the term *opiphobia* – the fear that one is becoming an epiphenomenalist.

175

362 THE PROBLEM OF OTHER MINDS

THE PROBLEM of other minds is a skeptical challenge that asks how we can be sure that other people have minds, given that we do not have access to their internal mental states. We cannot simply appeal to the fact that they exhibit complex behaviors, because we can imagine sophisticated robots, or philosophical zombies, exhibiting the same in the absence of mentality.

The standard response to this challenge is the argument from analogy. This holds that two facts together allow us to infer the existence of other minds: (a) all human beings have a similar physiological makeup; and (b) other people respond as I do in similar sorts of circumstances. Thus, for example, if I burn myself cooking, I will experience pain, and likely cry out. If other people do the same thing, they too will cry out with pain. It is reasonable to infer from the fact that we share the same physiology, that they too experience pain, and that therefore they must have a mind like ours.

Are you thinking what I'm thinking?

363 PERSONAL IDENTITY AND THE PERSISTENCE PROBLEM

🎓 **THE PERSISTENCE PROBLEM,** as it relates to personal identity, asks what it means to say that the same person exists at two (or more) different times. In one sense, it seems obvious that I am the same person today as I was a year ago; or that in the future I will be able to claim truthfully that I am the person who wrote this book. However, when it comes to identifying exactly what is required for it to be true that a person has persisted across time, things rapidly become very difficult.

Consider, for example, the claim that memory is key (as, for example, John Locke believed); that is, a person can be said to be you in the future if, and only if, they can remember the experiences you are having now. This formulation runs into the following problem. First, imagine a young racing driver is banned from racing. Later, as a mechanic, he remembers serving his ban. Finally, in old age, he remembers his career as a mechanic, but nothing about the ban or being a racing driver. If memory is key, it seems that the young racing driver is the middle-aged mechanic, the middle-aged mechanic is the old man, but the young racing driver isn't the old man. This clearly cannot be (because if x is identical to y, and y is identical to z, then x must also be identical to z).

364 FAST FACT...

📖 **THE HUMAN** body constantly creates new cells as old cells die. So are we really the same person we were when we were born?

365 THE FISSION PROBLEM

THE FISSION PROBLEM affects those approaches to the issue of the persistence of identity over time that emphasize the importance of psychological continuity. Put simply, the problem is that it seems possible a person could end up psychologically continuous with two or more future people at the same time.

Suppose, for example, we had the technology to create exact replicas of brains and that two copies of your brain are created (destroying your original brain in the process). The new brains are then transplanted into new bodies. We now have two people – You 1 and You 2 – both of whom are psychologically continuous with you (they have exactly your memories, dispositions, etc). According to psychological criterion, you are You 1 and you are also You 2. But this is impossible, because You 1 and You 2 are two things, and you are one thing, and two things cannot be identical to one thing.

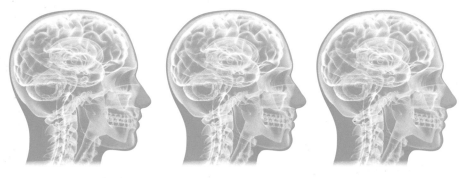

YOU   YOU 1   YOU 2

366 FAST FACT...

 **JOHN LOCKE** believed that personal identity (psychological continuity) was founded, not on the soul or the body, but on consciousness.

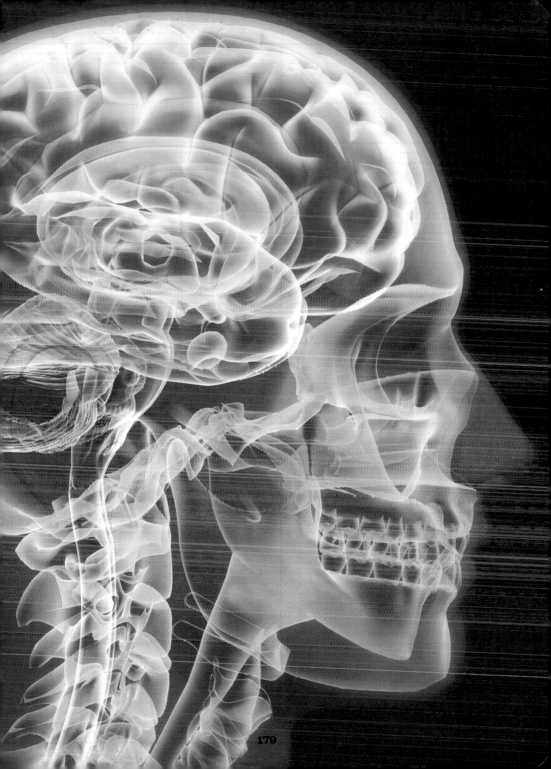

367 ANIMALISM

ANIMALISM is the view that the best answer to the question *"what kind of thing are we?"* is that we are human animals. In contrast to the orthodox view (associated with philosophers such as Derek Parfit), which holds that personal identity is in some way located in the mind, animalism asserts that it is the continuity of the body that is necessary for a person to persist across time.

Perhaps the major problem faced by animalism is explaining what is going on in those instances where it seems the person and the human animal have come apart (which is clearly impossible if they are one and the same thing). Take, for example, the case of somebody in a persistent vegetative state. Here the most plausible view seems to be that there is no person present, even though the human animal lives on.

Animalists are forced to deny this presumption. Thus, for example, Paul Snowdon argues that we do not really believe that if someone is in a vegetative state they are not a person. So, for instance, if we tried to visit a coma patient in hospital, only to be told we couldn't because the person we used to know wasn't there any more, we would be rightly perplexed.

368 FAST FACT...

METAPHYSICAL solipsists argue that the world outside one's own mind cannot be known and indeed might be non-existent.

369 THE BRAIN TRANSPLANT PROBLEM

🎓 **CONSIDER THE FOLLOWING** scenario, put forward by the philosopher Bernard Williams. Two people are about to undergo an odd experience. The thoughts and memories of Person A will be extracted from their brain, which will then be wiped clean. The same thing will happen to Person B. Then the memories and thoughts of Person A will be transmitted into the brain of the body that was formerly B's, and the memories and thoughts of Person B will be transmitted into the brain of the body that was formerly A's. This means we'll now have Body-Person A with the thoughts and memories of B, and Body-Person B with the thoughts and memories of A.

After the experiment, one body-person will be rewarded, the other will be tortured. Assume that you are the original person A (i.e., your memories and thoughts are going to end up in Body-Person B), and that you don't want to be tortured. Who do you want to be rewarded?

If you choose Body-Person A, then you think personal identity tracks *bodily continuity*. If you choose Body-Person B, then you think personal identity tracks *psychological continuity*.

OK, you're A, I'm B...
No, wait...

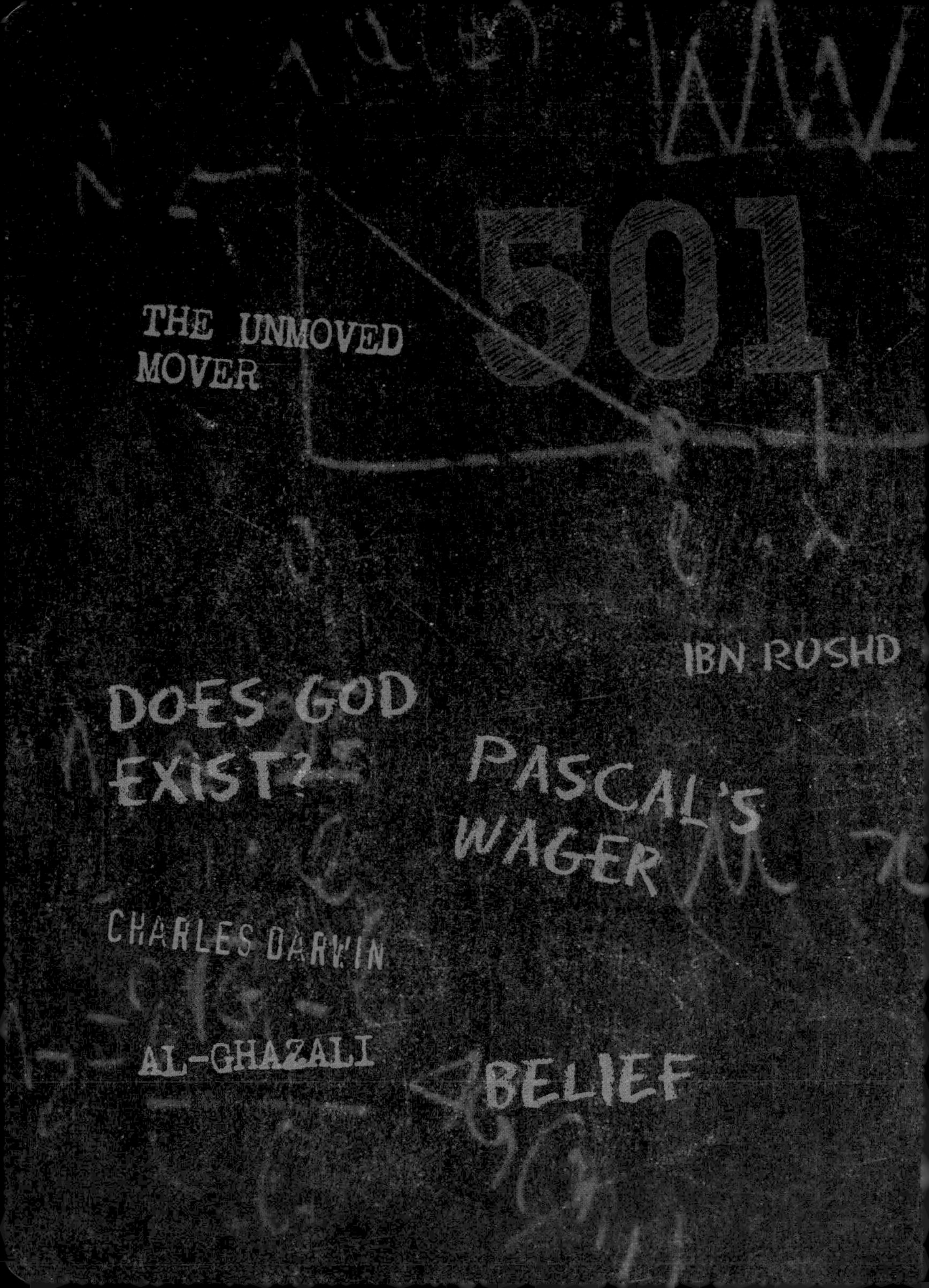

THE UNMOVED
MOVER

501

IBN RUSHD

DOES GOD
EXIST?

PASCAL'S
WAGER

CHARLES DARWIN

AL-GHAZALI

BELIEF

370 ONTOLOGICAL PROOF

👨‍🎓 **ANSELM OF CANTERBURY** outlined a proof of God that still puzzles philosophers to this day. Known as the ontological proof, it has the following form:

1. *God is "that than which nothing greater can be conceived."*

2. *God exists only in the mind or God exists in the mind and in reality.*

3. *Things that exist in the mind and in reality are greater than things that exist only in the mind.*

4. *If God exists only in the mind, then it is possible to conceive of something that is greater than God – namely, something that exists in the mind and in reality. However, God is "that than which nothing greater can be conceived". Therefore, God cannot exist only in the mind.*

5. *It follows, then, that God exists – both in the mind and in reality.*

You may feel that there is some trickery going on here, perhaps, for example, that the argument assumes what it sets out to prove. Nevertheless, the proof is persuasive enough to still interest philosophers today.

371 FAST FACT...

📖 **ANSELM'S** ontological proof appears in the second and third chapter of his *Proslogion*, a work in which he documents how the idea of God became self-evident to him.

372 FAST FACT...

📖 **ANSELM** was exiled from England twice (1097–1100 and 1105–07) during the investiture controversy, a conflict between Church and state over control of Church appointments.

373 THE INCOHERENCE OF THE PHILOSOPHERS

ABU HAMID AL-GHAZALI, arguably the first great Muslim intellectual, believed that it is not possible to come to a direct understanding of God just by using the usual techniques of theology and philosophy. Accordingly, his signature work, *The Incoherence of the Philosophers*, is highly critical of thinkers, such as Ibn Sina, who thought that Aristotelian reason, or mere words, could be used to derive religious truths.

Instead, Al-Ghazali argued that the techniques of the mystics were key to unlocking the divine:

"I apprehended clearly that the mystics are men who had real experiences, not men of words...What remained for me was not to be attained by oral instruction and study, but only by immediate experience and by walking in the mystic way."

It was al-Ghazali's view that our ability to apprehend God is based upon the divine quality of the human soul. However, the soul tends to be corrupted by a love of the material world, putting God out of reach. The purpose of prayer and religious ritual is to redeem the soul, thereby opening up the possibility of divine communication.

374 FAST FACT...

📖 **IN HIS BOOK,** Al-Ghazali wrote that when fire and cotton are placed in contact, the cotton is burned directly by God, rather than by the fire.

375 FAST FACT...

📖 **SOME PHILOSOPHERS** believe that Al-Ghazali's critique of metaphysics is even more incisive and decisive than Kant's.

376 THE INCOHERENCE OF INCOHERENCE

🎓 **IBN RUSHD**, otherwise known as Averroes, advocated for philosophy at a time when the discipline was coming under considerable pressure from the strictures of Islamic orthodoxy.

His major work, *The Incoherence of Incoherence*, was a response to the criticisms al-Ghazali had levelled at philosophy in his *Incoherence of the Philosophers*. Ibn Rushd argued that philosophical argument about religious matters is commanded by God, and he denied that philosophy tends to produce results that are contrary to scripture. He noted that it had long been understood by Muslims that the Qur'an is open to more than one interpretation, which means that it could not be true that unorthodox opinions were necessarily irreligious.

Ibn Rushd's philosophy was not entirely defensive. For example, he produced a variety of arguments that aimed at proving the existence of God, one of which held that the fact that living things exhibit the features of design, and the fact that the universe suits the purposes of human beings, demonstrates God's reality.

377 FAST FACT...

📖 **THE INCOHERENCE** of *Incoherence* is considered Ibn Rushd's masterpiece, in which he tries to find harmony between faith and philosophy.

378 FAST FACT...

📖 **IBN RUSHD'S** work was not well received by Islamic scholars, but was welcomed by Christian scholars, giving rise to the school of Averroism.

379 UNMOVED MOVER

. . . .

🎓 **THOMAS AQUINAS'** Five Ways (*Quinque viæ*), which he set out in his *Summa Theologica*, are designed to prove that God exists (though he readily accepts they tell us nothing about the character of God). The First Way, sometimes known as the argument from motion, has the following form:

1. Some things are in motion.

2. If something is in motion, then it must have been moved by something else.

3. An infinite regress of movers is not possible.

4. Therefore, there must be a first unmoved mover, which is God.

The steps in this argument are relatively self-explanatory. In essence, it holds that things do not move under their own steam, therefore, movement requires an explanation. However, at some point in the explanation of movement, it is going to be necessary to posit an unmoved mover, because otherwise the explanation will end up in an infinite regress. The unmoved mover is God.

This sort of argument is known as a cosmological argument, since it takes the very existence of the universe as necessitating God.

380 FAST FACT...

📖 *"Therefore it is necessary to arrive at a first mover, put in motion by no other; and this everyone understands to be God."* – Thomas Aquinas (1225–1274)

381 THE UNCAUSED CAUSER

AQUINAS' SECOND WAY, sometimes known as the argument from efficient cause, also has the form of a cosmological argument. Its structure is very similar to that of the First Way:

1. In the world, there are things that are caused.

2. Nothing is its own cause, which means that everything is caused by something else.

3. It is impossible for a series of causes to extend to infinity.

4. Therefore, there must be an uncaused cause, which is God.

The difference between this argument and the First Way is quite subtle. In the First Way, Aquinas notes that there are things in the world that are in motion or changing, and argues that at some point the explanation for motion must terminate with a mover that is itself unmoved. In the Second Way argument, Aquinas ventures that there are things in the world that are caused to exist by other things, and reasons that ultimately there must be something whose own existence is uncaused. This uncaused causer is God.

382 FAST FACT...

"There is no case known (neither is it, indeed, possible) in which a thing is found to be the efficient cause of itself." – Thomas Aquinas

AQUINAS' THIRD WAY is arguably the most interesting of his three cosmological arguments. Its starting point is a distinction between contingent and necessary things. A thing is contingent if it is logically possible for it not to have existed (so, for example, people and books are examples of contingent things). A thing is necessary if it cannot not have existed – its existence is a logical necessity (so, for example, the axioms of mathematics might be thought to be necessary things). With this distinction in mind, it is possible to see how Aquinas's Third Way argument works:

1. In the world, there are contingent things;

2. If everything in the universe were contingent, then there would have been a time when there was nothing.

3. However, if there was once nothing, then there would still be nothing, since there would be nothing to bring anything into existence.

4. Therefore, there must be a necessary being that is the cause of itself, and not dependent on any other being.

5. This is God.

384 FAST FACT...

📖 **IN THE 18TH CENTURY**, both David Hume and Immanuel Kant criticized Aquinas' cosmological argument (the first three ways).

385 FAST FACT...

📖 **IN THE GOD DELUSION**, Richard Dawkins dismisses the first three ways as essentially the same, relying on the idea of an infinite regress and assuming that God is immune to this.

386 THE ARGUMENT FROM DEGREE

THE ARGUMENT FROM DEGREE, Aquinas' Fourth Way, is a version of what is known as the moral argument for God, which aims to demonstrate God's existence from the fact that morality (apparently) exists in the world. Aquinas' argument holds that *"there must be something which is to all beings the cause of their being, goodness, and every other perfection: and this we call God."* More formally, the argument can be stated as follows:

1. There are differing degrees of perfection in the world.

2. The idea of a degree of perfection only makes sense against some ultimate standard of perfection.

3. Therefore, perfection must have an apex.

4. This is God.

This moral argument for God remains popular to this day. For example, the philosopher and theologian, William Lane Craig, defends a version of the argument that has the following form: if God does not exist, then objective moral values do not exist. Objective moral values do exist. Therefore, God exists.

387 FAST FACT...

THE ARGUMENT from Degree, Dawkins argues, could apply to any number of unrelated concepts, besides God.

388 FAST FACT...

PHILOSOPHER Paul Almond criticizes the Argument from Degree, saying one cannot prove that an object exists based only on the possibility that it exists.

389 THE TELEOLOGICAL ARGUMENT

🎓 **TELEOLOGICAL ARGUMENTS** for God's existence suggest that the universe exhibits a purposefulness that only makes sense if it is created and designed by God. Thomas Aquinas' Fifth Way holds that the universe is moving towards some specific end in the same way *"as an arrow is directed by the archer."* His argument works as follows:

1. There are things in the world that act towards specific goals.

2. These things do not have intelligence.

3. Acting towards a goal requires intelligence.

4. Therefore, a guiding intelligence exists.

5. This guiding intelligence is God.

Teleological arguments are inductive arguments in that they posit God as the best explanation for the (apparent) order and purpose exhibited by the universe. This means they are vulnerable to any alternative explanation that is able to explain this order and purpose. This vulnerability was thrown into sharp relief by the rise of modern science, and in particular by the emergence of Darwin's theory of natural selection.

390 FAST FACT...

📖 **DAWKINS** says that the Teleological Argument is no longer applicable because of what we have learned about evolution by natural selection.

391 FAST FACT...

📖 **PHILOSOPHER** Keith Ward argues that Aquinas's five ways only constitute a proof of God if one begins with the proposition that the universe can be rationally understood.

392 SCHOLASTICISM

THOMAS AQUINAS' *Summa Theologica* is arguably the highpoint of *scholasticism*, a method of argument and debate (or disputation) that dominated the medieval institutions of learning in Europe for several hundred years.

393 FAST FACT...

📖 **SCHOLASTICISM** emerged through the recovery of Greek philosophical writings in the 10th–13th centuries, after these had been lost to the Latin West.

Scholasticism has a bad reputation in the present day. The problem is the notoriously insular character of many of its concerns, satirized in the notion that the scholastics spent most of their time trying to figure out how many angels it is possible to get on the head of a pin. Ironically, it is likely that nobody actually considered that precise issue, but when you consider that Aquinas's *Summation of Theology* contains 358 questions and answers about angels, you can see that the objection has merit.

Unfortunately, this interest in the minutiae of religious doctrine had negative effects on philosophy, which during the heyday of scholasticism effectively became a branch of theology. Scholastic philosophers were, in a sense, the masters of rational argument. However, it was rational argument almost exclusively employed in the service of religious belief.

394 FAST FACT...

📖 **SCHOLASTIC** debate continues today through Internet discussion groups such as Aquinas and Thomism. The scholastic method is still used by some analytic philosophers.

395 PASCAL'S WAGER

🎓 **BLAISE PASCAL** was not always a deeply religious man. However, on the night of November 23 1654, he had a conversion experience that was so intense he recorded it on a sheet of parchment, which he then had sewn into his coat.

Pascal is best known in the present day for the "wager" argument that appears in his work *Pensées*. The argument is as follows. Either God exists or he does not. This is an unavoidable existential question, which requires us to choose one way or the other. If God does not exist, then we do not lose much by erroneously thinking he does exist. If God does exist, then we stand to gain a lot by (correctly) thinking he does, and stand to lose everything by thinking he does not. Therefore, it is rational to believe in God, and to behave in accordance with this belief.

The wager is not an argument for the existence of God, such as those of Thomas Aquinas. It is an argument for the rationality of *belief in* God.

398 ON DESIGN

🎓 **YOU ARE WALKING** across a field when you notice a watch on the ground. You pick it up and admire the complexity of its design and the intricacy of its workings. You recognize that there is no way it could have come about by chance. It manifests order and regularity, and clearly has been put together to fulfil some purpose. From this it is possible to infer that it must have had a maker.

Now consider how much less complex a watch is than the human eye. If a watch could not have sprung together by chance, then it is unimaginable that something as complex and highly wrought as the eye could have arisen simply as a consequence of natural mechanisms. The eye is just too highly specified to be anything other than the creation of an intelligent designer.

This is a version of an argument outlined by William Paley in his book, *Natural Theology*. It aims to show by means of an argument from analogy that the universe, which manifests extraordinary complexity, order and regularity, must have had a designer. The designer, of course, turns out to be God.

399 FAST FACT...

📖 **AS A THEOLOGY STUDENT**, Charles Darwin believed that Paley had provided rational proof of the existence of God. His later studies changed his mind.

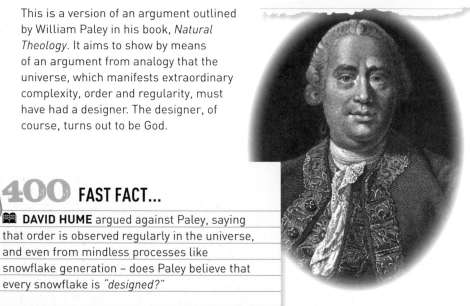

400 FAST FACT...

📖 **DAVID HUME** argued against Paley, saying that order is observed regularly in the universe, and even from mindless processes like snowflake generation – does Paley believe that every snowflake is *"designed?"*

401 DARWIN ON NATURAL SELECTION

🎓 **CHARLES DARWIN'S** theory of natural selection shows precisely how the sort of "design" that Paley identified could have come about without the intervention of an intelligent designer.

According to Darwin, life in the natural world is characterized by a relentless struggle for existence – or, more precisely, for reproduction – because any species will tend to produce more individuals than can be sustained. It was this insight that led him to his theory of evolution by natural selection.

Charles Darwin

Every species manifests some variation in the inherited traits of its members. Take foxes, for example: some foxes will be able to run faster than other foxes; some will have better eyesight, better hearing, sharper teeth, and better camouflage. Variations that give an individual a competitive advantage (sharper teeth and better eyesight) will tend to be passed on more often than variations that put an individual at a disadvantage (e.g. a birthmark that makes its bearer a sitting target). Therefore, given enough time, helpful variations will come to be much more numerous than less helpful variations. So long as there are always new variations for natural selection to operate upon, then evolution will carry on in this way indefinitely.

402 FAST FACT...

📖 *"We can no longer argue that, for instance, the beautiful hinge of a bivalve shell must have been made by an intelligent being, like the hinge of a door by man."* – Charles Darwin (1809–1882)

This is a hugely powerful idea. It answers Paley's challenge, explaining how the eye could have emerged naturalistically by means of tiny, incremental steps, each one beneficial in its own right.

ON THE ORIGIN OF SPECIES (1859)

DARWIN'S THEORY OF EVOLUTION is built on several fundamental core ideas, which were put forward in the publication of *On the Origin of Species by Means of Natural Selection* in 1859.

FIRSTLY was the observation that species change over time and space, that is to say that members of particular species living today will be different to those living in the past, and to those living in a different geographical area. Fossils are a good example of this principle at work.

SECONDLY, Darwin proposed that all organisms share a common ancestor. Over time, populations may divide into different species but will remain distantly related to an ancestor who passed on certain physical or behavioral traits.

Darwin believed that the main mechanism for change over time was natural selection, which he broke into four parts:

VARIATION: Within populations, organisms will exhibit individual variations, for example body size, markings or hair color.

INHERITANCE: Some traits are passed on from a parent to its offspring. These are heritable traits. Other traits that have a strong environmental basis show weak heritability.

Let's get started!

198

POPULATION GROWTH: Each year, most populations produce more offspring than their environment can support, leading to a fight for resources or "struggle for existence."

SURVIVAL AND REPRODUCTION: Individuals who possess traits that help them in the fight for resources will survive and produce more offspring for the next generation, passing on the advantageous heritable traits or adaptations (the "survival of the fittest.")

In the twentieth century, scientists made significant advancements in the field of genetics and were able to link gene theory with Darwin's earlier arguments. The hereditary traits passed on from one generation to the next were found to be chance mutations on a certain part of the genetic code for the trait. Advantageous mutations lead to a higher chance of survival and successful reproduction, thus passing on the mutations to the new offspring. Over time, advantageous traits become more and more common in a population.

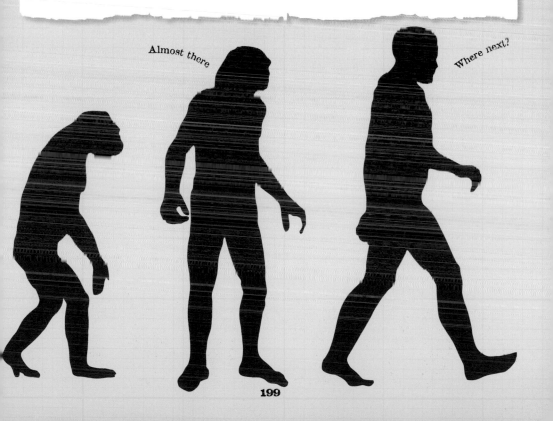

Almost there

Where next?

403 THE EUTHYPHRO DILEMMA

THE EUTHYPHRO DILEMMA arises out of the following question: does God command what is good because it is good; or is it good simply because it is commanded by God?

Whichever way you answer this question, you run into difficulties. If you respond that God commands what it is good because it is good, then you risk ending up with a diminished God, because the response seems to imply that there are moral standards independent of God's will. This threatens God's authority, (since he will not have control over the domain of morals), and his independence (because his own goodness is dependent upon the extent to which he conforms to independent moral standards.)

However, the opposite response (that the good is good just because God commands it) has its own set of problems. In particular, it seems to make morality arbitrary, just a matter of God's whim. Consider, for example, that God might wake up one morning and decide that adultery is now obligatory. If the good is good just because God commands it, and God has freedom of will, then it seems there is nothing to rule this out.

404 FAST FACT...

📖 JEWISH PHILOSOPHERS

Avi Sagi and Daniel Statman criticized the Euthyphro Dilemma, saying it leaves out a third option, namely that God *"acts only out of His nature."*

405 THE PROBLEM OF EVIL

🎓 **THE PROBLEM OF EVIL** refers to the difficulty of explaining the presence of evil in the world, given the existence of a God that is all-powerful, all-knowing and wholly good.

It is often claimed that Epicurus was responsible for the first statement of the problem of evil:

"God...either wishes to take away evils, and is unable; or He is able, and is unwilling; or He is neither willing nor able, or He is both willing and able. If He is willing and is unable, He is feeble, which is not in accordance with the character of God; if He is able and unwilling, He is envious, which is equally at variance with God; if He is neither willing nor able, He is both envious and feeble, and therefore not God; if He is both willing and able, which alone is suitable to God, from what source then are evils? Or why does He not remove them?"

406 FAST FACT...

📖 *"It [God] wants to [abolish evil], but cannot, he is impotent. If he can, but does not want to, he is wicked."*
– Epicurus (341–270 BC)

In essence, the argument here is that God ought to be both willing and able to eradicate evil from the world. Therefore, given that there is evil in the world, it appears God is either unwilling or unable (or both) to do so. If he is unable, then he is weak; if he is unwilling, then he is not wholly good.

The image of the Three Wise Monkeys originated in Japan. They embody the maxim "See no evil, hear no evil, speak no evil."

407 THE ARGUMENT FROM RELIGIOUS EXPERIENCE

PEOPLE HAVE CLAIMED to experience the divine in various ways for as long as religion has been in existence. The exemplary case in the Western tradition is perhaps Paul's Damascene experience, which (allegedly) struck him blind for three days and prompted his conversion to Christianity.

The key issue in determining whether religious experience constitutes evidence for the existence of the divine is its veridicality; that is to say, whether it corresponds to anything outside the mind of the person having the experience.

In his book, *The Existence of God*, Richard Swinburne argues that two principles should govern how we view religious experience. The principle of credulity holds that in the absence of a reason to disbelieve it, we have good reason to suppose that what we experience is actually what is there; and the principle of testimony asserts that, provided there are no special considerations in play (such as a person being drunk), we should not doubt what people report in their testimonies. These two principles together add up to the claim that unless there are specific reasons *not* to believe reports of religious experience, then we should accept that if people say they have experienced something, they have experienced it.

St Paul the Apostle on the road to Damascus. The Bible tells that he saw a blinding light and heard a divine voice.

408 THE NEW ATHEISM

🎓 **THE NEW ATHEISM** is an assertive form of atheism that has emerged primarily in English-speaking countries in the last decade. The birth of the movement is normally dated from the publication of four books: *The End of Faith* by Sam Harris; *The God Delusion* by Richard Dawkins; *Breaking the Spell* by Daniel Dennett; and *God is Not Great* by Christopher Hitchens.

There is nothing particularly novel about the ideas espoused by New Atheist authors, and the arguments they make are not especially sophisticated. Nevertheless, there is no doubt that New Atheism has brought secular ideas to the attention of a vast number of people, perhaps more numerous than at any other period in history.

There is no evidence as yet that New Atheism is having a significant effect on the level of religious belief in the English-speaking world, and it remains to be seen whether the increased cultural space that has been carved out for secular ideas remains open.

409 FAST FACT...

📖 **THE NEW ATHEISTS** consider religious claims (e.g. the virgin birth, miracles and the afterlife) as legitimate questions for scientific enquiry.

410 FAST FACT...

📖 **ON HIS WEBSITE,** Richard Dawkins refers to himself, Sam Harris, Daniel Dennett and Christopher Hitchens as "The Four Horsemen."

Does New Atheism mark the beginning of the end for religious belief?

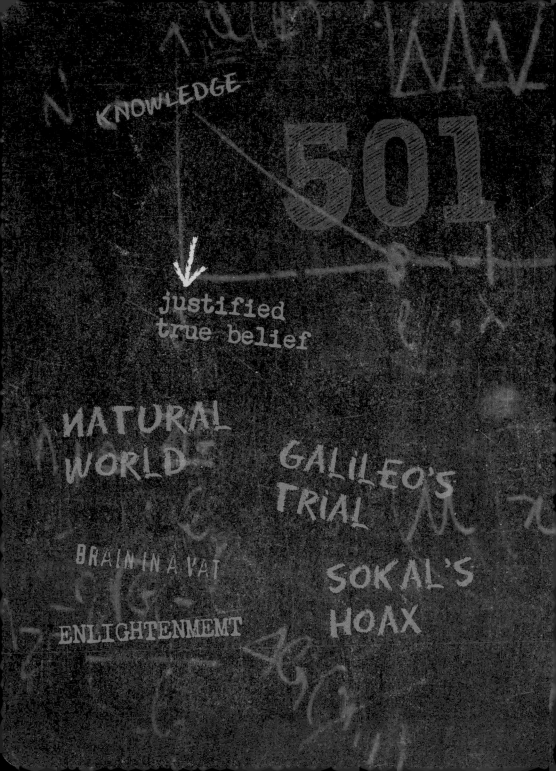

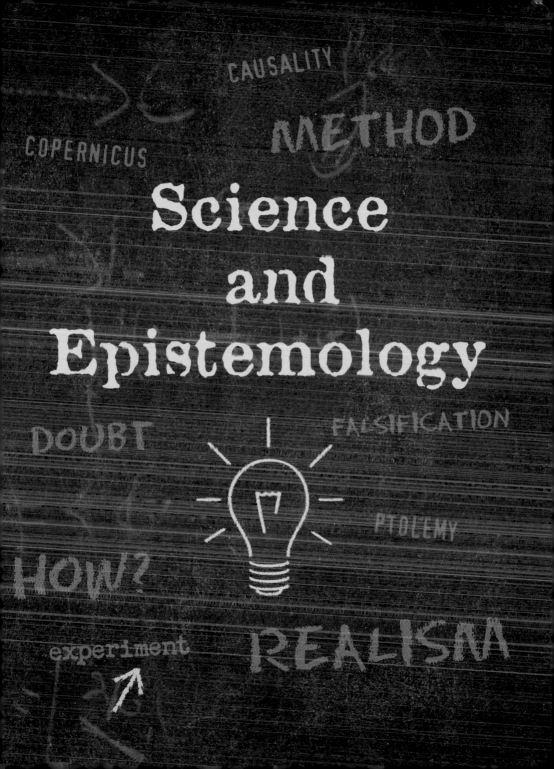

411 ARISTOTLE AND THE NATURAL WORLD

🎓 **ARISTOTLE'S ATTEMPT** to understand the natural world was not as successful as his more properly philosophical endeavors. In this regard, he is not so very different from his Ancient Greek colleagues, except such was his influence on the intellectual development of Christian Europe that his errors came to have serious consequences.

412 FAST FACT...

📖 *"All men by nature desire knowledge."* – Aristotle (384–322 BC)

Perhaps the most significant way in which Aristotle went awry was in seeing *purpose* as being woven into the fabric of the world. In contrast to the atomists, who sought to explain the world in mechanistic terms, Aristotle thought that at least part of the explanation of objects and events was the purpose towards which they were directed. Bertrand Russell points out that Aristotle could not really have known that this was the wrong way to look at things. Nevertheless, the consequence of looking for *teleological* rather than mechanistic explanations of natural phenomena was that science ended up going down a blind alley until at least the Renaissance.

413 BACON'S SCIENTIFIC METHOD

🎓 **FRANCIS BACON,** who was born into minor nobility in Elizabethan England, was responsible for the first statement of something akin to a scientific method. He argued that a sophisticated form of induction, which looks at the circumstances in which a phenomenon occurs, and the circumstances in which it does not occur, could form the basis of a reliable science.

Bacon uses the example of heat to illustrate his idea. Suppose we have noted that although water is normally inert, it is seen to boil at high temperatures and freezes at low temperatures. This might lead us to hypothesize that other liquids will behave in a similar way if they are heated or frozen. So we could try boiling oil, or freezing mercury. Eventually, given enough observations, it's likely we would be able to infer a general law describing the behavior of heat in liquids.

This is not science proper, but it is a huge step forward when compared to the haphazard investigations of the natural world that characterized Bacon's time.

Francis Bacon (1561–1626)

414 FAST FACT...

📖 **ISAAC NEWTON** was a noted Baconian. In saying, *"Hypotheses non fingo"* (I feign no hypotheses), he meant that he preferred rules that could be demonstrated by formal proof.

415 PTOLEMY VERSUS COPERNICUS

🎓 **IN MANY WAYS,** the seventeenth-century emergence of the Copernican heliocentric model of the universe as a serious alternative to the Ptolemaic geocentric system marks the beginnings of the modern era.

Geocentrism is the idea that the Earth lies at the center of the universe and every other heavenly body orbits around it. This idea was common in Ancient Greece, and Aristotle developed a fully developed version of the theory. However, it was Claudius Ptolemy in the second century who laid down the system that became the standard Geocentric model. This went on to dominate cosmological ideas in the Christian and Islamic worlds for more than a millennium.

It was not until the publication of Nicholas Copernicus's *On the Revolutions of the Heavenly Spheres* in 1543 that the Ptolemaic system came under serious pressure. Copernicus's theory had the sun at the center of things, and the Earth and the other planets revolving around it. At first, Copernicus's model was not taken too seriously, because its predictions were no more accurate than those of the Ptolemaic system. However, this all changed when Galileo stepped onto the stage.

416 FAST FACT...

📖 **THE FIRST** person known to have proposed a heliocentric system was Aristarchus of Samos (c. 270 BC).

417 GALILEO'S TRIAL

IN 1609, the great Italian scientist and mathematician, Galileo, made a series of observations that seemed to support the Copernican heliocentric view of the universe. This did not please the Catholic Church, which held that the Bible endorsed geocentrism, and Galileo was ordered to keep quiet.

This he did for a little while, but in the mid-1620s, he returned to the issue again, and began to work on the book that would be published in 1632 as *Dialogue Concerning the Two Chief World Systems*. This work made it clear that Galileo believed the Copernican model, rather than the old Ptolemaic orthodoxy, accurately described the universe.

The Catholic Church, under Pope Urban VII, was not amused by this turn of events. In April 1633, Galileo was summoned to appear before the Inquisition, and he was found *"vehemently suspect of heresy,"* required to *"abjure, curse and detest"* his heretical opinions, and sentenced to house arrest for the remainder of his life.

The Catholic Church did not formally drop its opposition to heliocentrism until the 1820s; and it was not until the late twentieth century that it finally apologized for the harm it had done to Galileo.

418 FAST FACT...

AT GALILEO'S TRIAL, a commission of theologians gave their verdict on heliocentrism as *"foolish and absurd in philosophy, and formally heretical since it explicitly contradicts ... the sense of Holy Scripture."*

419 FAST FACT...

AFTER RECEIVING his guilty verdict, Galileo is said to have muttered the rebellious phrase *"And yet it moves,"* speaking of the Earth.

421 THE ENLIGHTENMENT

🎓 **ACCORDING TO IMMANUEL KANT**, the Enlightenment – an intellectual movement that rose to prominence in Western Europe during the seventeenth and eighteenth centuries – marked the *"emergence of man from this self-imposed infancy."*

Man's infancy was characterized by a religious hegemony, which insisted that all questions about the nature of the universe and the place of human beings in it had to be answered in terms that would be sanctioned by religious authority (hence the row over Galileo's heliocentrism). It was against this background that thinkers such as John Locke in England and Voltaire in France began to give voice to the Enlightenment message. In general terms, this emphasized the essentially *rational* character of human beings, and promoted the idea that everybody had the ability to use *reason* to find out about the world and to progress morally.

Enlightenment thinkers tended to be either deists or atheists, but preached religious tolerance. In fact, tolerance was a central Enlightenment value. Voltaire, for example, wrote a *Treatise on Tolerance*, in which he advocated for *"a universal tolerance"* of all peoples and religions on the grounds that *"we should regard all men as our brothers."*

422 FAST FACT...

📖 **THE TERM** Enlightenment did not come into use in English until the mid-eighteenth century, a century after the movement first began.

423 FAST FACT...

📖 **KANT** called the Enlightenment *"Mankind's final coming of age, the emancipation of the human consciousness from an immature state of ignorance and error."*

424 HUME ON CAUSALITY

🎓 **DAVID HUME** is the exemplary skeptical philosopher. Perhaps the most striking of his skeptical arguments is the one he developed to undermine the standard way we think about causality (that is, cause and effect).

It was Hume's view that the causal relations we discern in the world are uncovered by a process of induction. If a billiard ball hits another billiard ball, which then moves, we will tend to say that the first ball caused the movement of the second. Hume argues that we are able to make this inference because we have seen this sort of thing happen many times before. In other words, we assume the world will manifest the same cause and effect conjunctions over and over again.

However, Hume's rather disturbing point is that there is nothing that makes these conjunctions logical necessities, which means there is no contradiction in asserting that a billiard ball will not move the next time it is struck (even if it has moved on every previous occasion). Or, to put this more generally, there is nothing about past behavior or events that makes their re-occurrence necessary in the future, even under identical circumstances,.

425 FAST FACT...

📖 **HUME** himself rarely used the term induction. It was John Maynard Keynes in the early twentieth century who first associated Hume with this method.

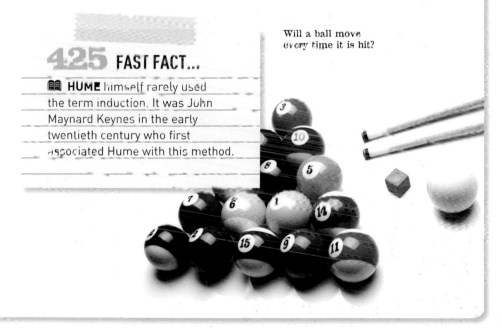

Will a ball move every time it is hit?

426 HUME ON MIRACLES

ALTHOUGH HUME does not rule out the possibility of miracles as a matter of principle, he denies that there has ever been an event that could reasonably be thought of as a miracle. The reason for his skepticism is essentially a matter of probability.

We know that if miracles occur then they are extremely rare. We also recognize that there has never been a generally accepted occurrence of a miracle (even if we are tempted ourselves to believe in particular miracles). In light of these two considerations, the appropriate response to any claim that somebody has witnessed an event that necessitated a suspension of the laws of nature is extreme skepticism. The question we need to ask ourselves is whether it is more likely that a person's testimony is a mistake, or fraudulent, or whether it is more likely that the laws of nature have been suspended. Everything we know about human nature and about the natural world tells us that it is more likely the testimony is false. It follows, then, that there are no good grounds for thinking that a miracle has occurred.

427 FAST FACT...

ACCORDING TO SOME CRITICS, Hume's argument against miracles is circular. He says that the laws of nature are supported by exceptionless testimony, but testimony can only be exceptionless if we discount the occurrence of miracles.

428 KNOWLEDGE AS JUSTIFIED TRUE BELIEF

THE ISSUE of what counts as knowledge is tricky. Suppose, for example, that you have a particularly vivid dream about aliens, and afterwards you start telling everybody that there is life on other planets. As it happens, there is life on other planets, and a little while after your dream, aliens make contact with Earth, and set up a camp outside The White House.

In this situation, you might be tempted to insist you were right to claim that you knew aliens existed. However, most philosophers would consider such a claim to be highly dubious. The problem is that although as it turned out that your belief that aliens existed was true, the belief itself was not justified. In other words, you did not have rational grounds for believing that aliens existed.

If it is not clear why a belief has to be true and justified to count as knowledge, consider the following example. A man buys a lottery ticket, claiming he knows that he is going to win despite the odds being stacked 14 million to 1 against him. As it turns out, he does win. In this sort of situation, most people will not believe that he really *knew* that he was going to win. They will think he had the *belief* he was going to win, and then he got lucky.

429 SCIENTIFIC METHOD

SCIENCE, properly understood, is not a body of knowledge, but rather a method for finding out about the world that emphasizes the importance of observation, hypothesis formation, testing, theory generation and peer review. The scientific method is sometimes specified more formally in terms of a schema that takes the following form:

1. Identify problems, define questions.
2. Perform observations, gather data, identify resources.
3. Develop hypotheses.
4. Generate testable propositions.
5. Test propositions (via experiments).
6. Accept or reject experimental hypotheses.
7. Report results (so that they can be tested and reviewed by the scientific community as a whole).

The reality of science is both more creative and more chaotic than this type of schema allows. Nevertheless, the success of the scientific method comes down to its ability to let the data speak for itself. It does not matter what we *want* to be true, results either confirm hypotheses or they do not.

430 FAST FACT...

IN EXPERIENCE *and Nature,* Dewey argued that much of the debate about the relation of the mind to the body results from conceptual confusions.

431 FAST FACT...

JOHN DEWEY was a radical empiricist who wanted to give a place to meaning and value instead of explaining them away as subjective additions to a world of whizzing atoms.

432 FAST FACT...

THE TERM empiricism derives from the Greek *empeiria*, meaning experience.

433 FAST FACT...

DEWEY criticized the view of education as a means to an end. He viewed it not as a preparation for life but as life itself.

434 POPPER ON FALSIFICATION

KARL POPPER argued that the ability of science to generate hypotheses that can be falsified is the main reason it is so successful as a method for finding out about the world. To understand what is involved in this claim, consider the following example. You have become convinced that all swans are white, so you go around counting white swans with the aim of demonstrating the proof of your contention. However, it occurs to you that actually your rationale is flawed. It doesn't matter how many white swans you count, you can never rule out the possibility that the next swan you find will be black. As Popper puts it, *"no matter how many instances of white swans we may have observed, this does not justify the conclusion that all swans are white."*

However, though we cannot prove that all swans are white by counting white swans, we can certainly falsify the proposition. All we have to do is to find one instance of a black swan. This point has implications for the way that science should proceed. It was Popper's view that science proper has to generate propositions that can be tested and falsified. If a particular discipline does not generate falsifiable proposition, then it is not a science. Thus, for example, he criticized Freudian theory on the grounds that there is no way to falsify its central claims.

435 FAST FACT...

FALSIFIABILITY has been used in court as a means of distinguishing science from non-science. Creationism is unfalsifiable, because it relies on faith, and would therefore be regarded by Popper as non-science.

436 THE STRUCTURE OF SCIENTIFIC REVOLUTIONS

🎓 **IN HIS RENOWNED,** *The Structure of Scientific Revolutions*, Thomas Kuhn argues that "normal science" proceeds according to the requirements of specific "paradigms" that define the rules and standards of scientific practice for any specific scientific field.

According to Kuhn, the history of science is marked by occasional "scientific revolutions" that see the dominant paradigm in a particular field being replaced by a new paradigm (as, for example, occurred in the case of geocentrism and heliocentrism). A scientific revolution is sparked by a period of crisis, during which it becomes obvious that an existing paradigm can no longer be sustained in the face of a growing number of puzzles and difficulties. The revolution occurs when the scientific community as a whole shifts over to the new paradigm, which brings an end to the crisis, allowing normal science to resume.

It is often thought that Kuhn's arguments imply that there can be no real progress in science (since any particular paradigm is destined to be overthrown). However, his view was that modern scientific theories are better than earlier ones in that they are able to solve a larger number of puzzles under a greater variety of conditions.

437 FAST FACT...

📖 **SOME ACCUSED** Kuhn of plagiarizing the work of Hungarian-British polymath Michael Polanyi. In response, Kuhn cited Polanyi in the second edition of his book.

438 FAST FACT...

📖 **KUHN'S** influential work popularized the terms *paradigm shift*, *normal science* and *scientific revolutions*.

439 REALISM VERSUS ANTI-REALISM

REALISM, or, more precisely, external realism, is the view that the world exists independently of our perceptions of it and also of our thoughts, attitudes and feelings about it. Realism also asserts that the world is knowable by us.

This view might seem unobjectionable, but in fact it is surrounded by choppy philosophical waters. Most objections to realism rely on the fact that we do not have direct, unmediated access to the external world. Anti-realists point out that our biology, brains, language, culture, history and concepts are all variously implicated in the way that we come to understand reality. There is no view from anywhere that enables us to take a God's eye perspective on the objects of our perception and understanding.

The anti-realist position comes with large costs. Consider, for example, that it seems to threaten tyranny and totalitarianism. If truth is not constrained by the nature of an independent reality, then truth-claims can be hijacked by powerful groups for political purposes. Thus, for instance, if a racist group were to claim that Aryans are a "superior race" and there is no independent criterion of truth, it is not obvious how the claim could be falsified.

440 FAST FACT...

MICHAEL DUMMETT, the British philosopher who popularized the term "anti-realism," also introduced a new type of voting system, the Quota Borda System.

441 RELATIVISM

PART OF THE CONCERN over the anti-realist position is that it appears to lead to relativism, which, broadly speaking, is the claim that propositions are only true or false in relation to particular cultures, discourses, language-games, paradigms, and so on.

It is easy to see how anti-realism can collapse into relativism. If there is no reality independent of our concepts, it follows that what is true in terms of one particular conceptual framework might not be true in terms of another, and that there will (probably) be no way of determining which of the two frameworks is to be preferred.

However, there is the consoling thought here that relativism is likely to be self-defeating. This has to do with what philosopher David Stove called the *"Ishmael effect."* The difficulty for relativism is that it seems to make an exception of itself. In other words, its claim that propositions are only true or false relatively, itself appears not to be a claim that is only true or false in relation to a particular conceptual framework or discourse.

The Ishmael effect is named after the narrator of *Moby Dick*

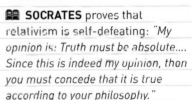

442 FAST FACT...

SOCRATES proves that relativism is self-defeating: *"My opinion is: Truth must be absolute.... Since this is indeed my opinion, then you must concede that it is true according to your philosophy."*

443 FAST FACT...

"To confuse our own constructions with eternal laws or divine decrees is one of the most fatal delusions of men."
– a relativistic view from Isaiah Berlin

444 BRAIN IN A VAT

🎓 **THE "BRAIN IN A VAT"** thought experiment is based on the idea that the experience of a simulated reality would be no different from the experience of the real thing. It asks us to imagine that a brain has been taken out of a person's head, put in a vat of fluid, and then connected to a device that entirely replicates the electrical impulses that usually come in from the outside world.
The contention is that such a device would create an experience of a simulated reality that would be indistinguishable from the real world.

This introduces the problem of radical skepticism. It seems you might already be living in such a situation, but not be aware of it. This would mean that all your current beliefs about the world are false. Right now, you are not reading this book at all. The experience is being created for you by a machine located in a lockup somewhere near Poughkeepsie.

445 FAST FACT...

📖 **THE BRAIN IN A VAT** idea has been a staple of science fiction dramas, including *Cold Lazarus*, *Donovan's Brain*, *The Matrix*, *Source Code*, *Inception*, *The Thirteenth Floor* and *Dark Star*.

446 SOKAL'S HOAX

THE PHYSICIST Alan Sokal hit the headlines in 1996, when he managed to persuade a leading cultural studies journal, *Social Text*, to publish what should have been an obviously spoof article. His motivation for writing the article was what he took to be a rise in *"sloppily thought out relativism,"* which had become the *"unexamined zeitgeist of large areas of the American humanities."*

Sokal's article, titled "Transgressing the Boundaries: Towards a Transformative Hermeneutics of Quantum Gravity," is not a particularly subtle parody. It begins by asserting (wrongly, of course) that most Western intellectuals no longer believe there is any such thing as the real world, and then goes on to mesh together deliberate mathematical errors and jokes with extensive quotations from doyens of postmodernism, such as Lacan and Irigaray. The article concludes with the claim that since physical reality is a construct, it is necessary to establish a liberatory science and emancipatory mathematics that could be allied to a progressive political project.

Sokal stresses that it is important not to read too much into the fact that one journal had terrible editorial standards. Nevertheless, the Sokal affair does provide the lesson that just because an article appears in an academic journal, and just because people claim to understand it, it does not follow that it actually makes sense!

447 FAST FACT...

SOKAL claimed he had undertaken the hoax to *"defend the Left from a trendy segment of itself."*

448 FAST FACT...

"But why did I do it? I confess that I'm an unabashed Old Leftist who never quite understood how deconstruction was supposed to help the working class."
– Alan Sokal (1955–)

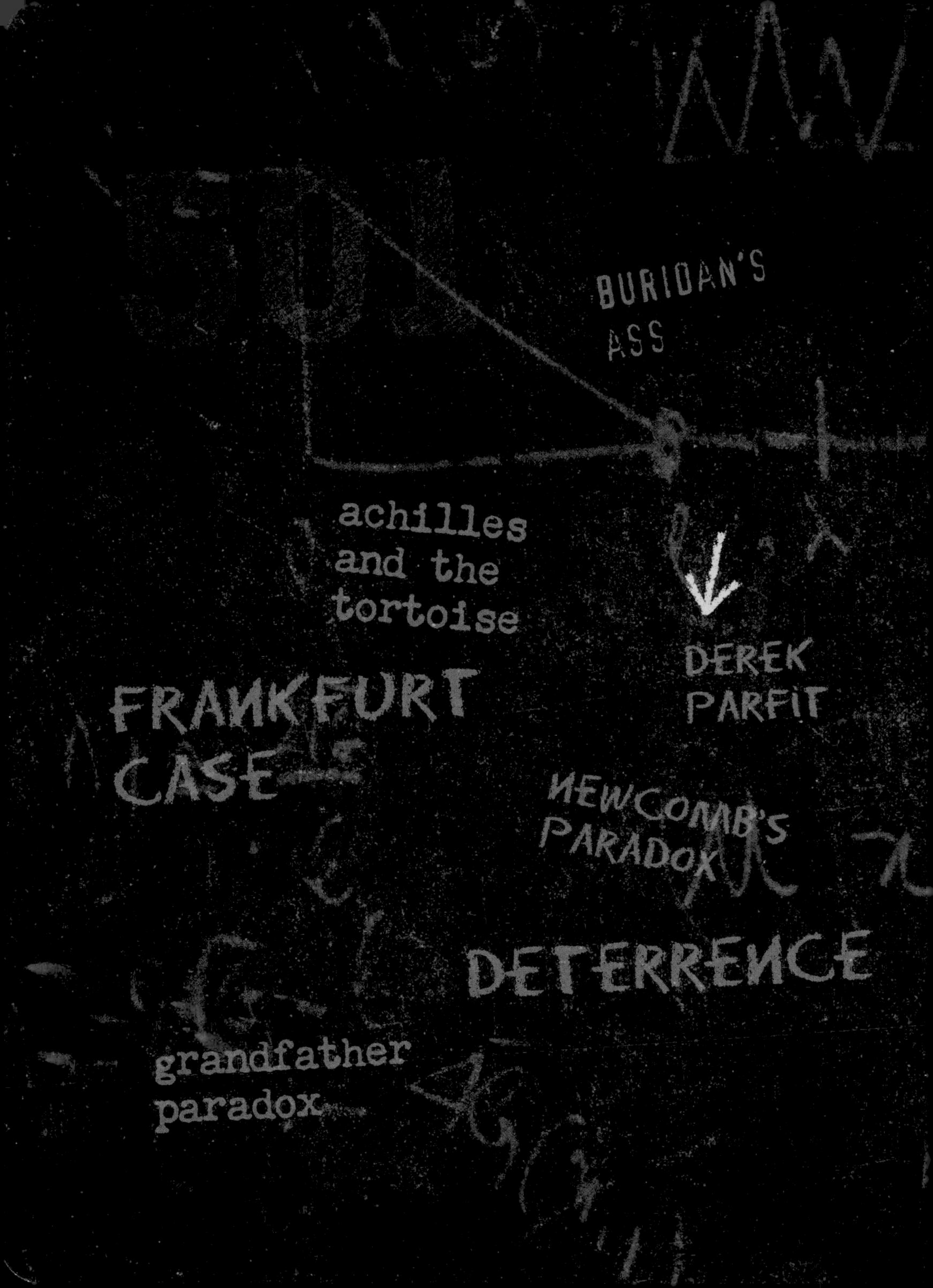

BURIDAN'S
ASS

achilles
and the
tortoise

DEREK
PARFIT

FRANKFURT
CASE

NEWCOMB'S
PARADOX

DETERRENCE

grandfather
paradox

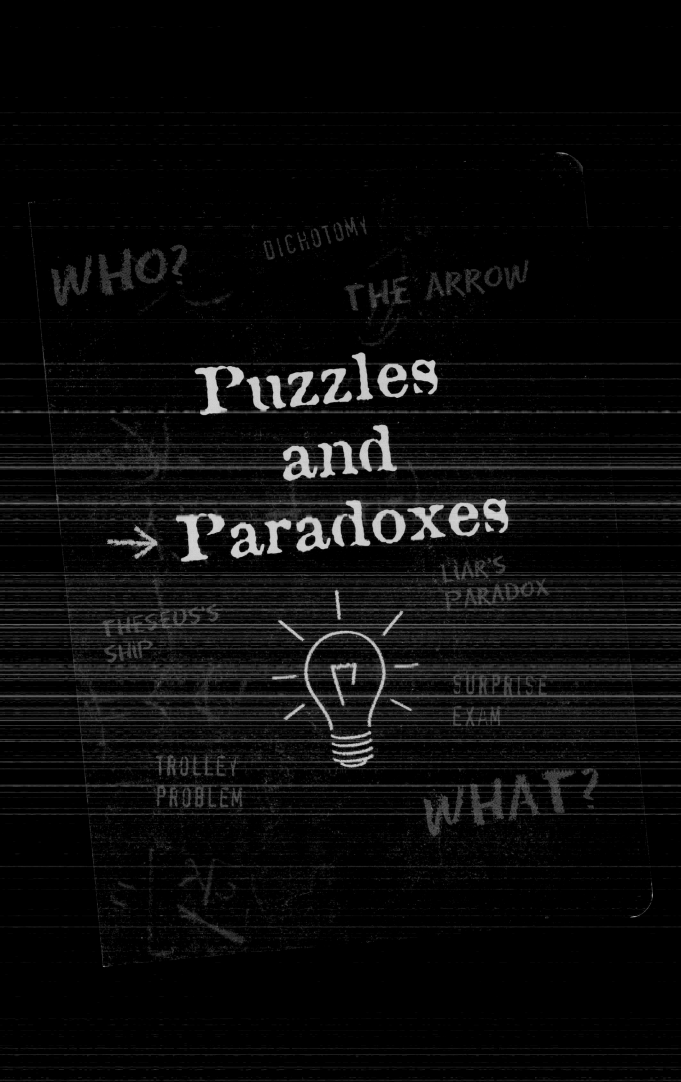

449 THE DICHOTOMY

🎓 **ACCORDING TO ARISTOTLE**, the first of Zeno of Elea's famous paradoxes *"asserts the non-existence of motion on the grounds that that which is in motion must arrive at the halfway stage before it arrives at the goal."*

450 FAST FACT...

📖 **ZENO'S** arguments are perhaps the first examples of a method of proof called *reductio ad absurdum* (reduce to the absurd).

At first, it may not be obvious why having to arrive at the halfway point on a journey would make motion impossible, but the argument itself is quite straightforward. If you want to cross a road, then it is necessary for you to cover half the distance before you can complete the journey. However, it is not possible to travel half the distance, until you cover half of half the distance, and you can't travel half of half the distance until you cover half of that distance, and so on, ad infinitum. This argument appears to show that your attempt to cross the road would never even get started. It seems that motion is impossible.

Of course, we know that motion is entirely possible, and that you would be able to cross the road. However, identifying exactly what is wrong with Zeno's argument is not easy!

451 FAST FACT...

📖 **ACCORDING** to Diogenes Laertius, Zeno of Elea was *"skilled to argue both sides of any question, the universal critic."*

452 ACHILLES AND THE TORTOISE

ACHILLES AND THE TORTOISE is probably the most famous of Zeno's paradoxes.

Achilles is taking on a tortoise in a race, but the tortoise is slow, so he gives her a head start. At the beginning of the race, the tortoise is in the lead, but Achilles rapidly closes the gap. First he gets to the point where the tortoise had started the race, only to find that the tortoise has moved on a little way. He aims to catch the tortoise at her new location, but when he arrives there he finds the tortoise has moved on a little further still. The race proceeds in this fashion, with Achilles getting ever closer to the tortoise, but never actually catching her, because whenever he reaches a point where the tortoise has been, the tortoise has moved on a bit further, even if only by a tiny distance.

It seems, then, that Achilles can never catch the tortoise, despite being a lot faster than his plodding rival. As with Zeno's first paradox, we know this conclusion is absurd, but where the reasoning goes wrong is not obvious.

453 FAST FACT...

ACCORDING TO PROCLUS, Zeno produced *"not less than 40 arguments revealing contradictions,"* but only nine of his paradoxes are now known.

454 FAST FACT...

THE PARADOX of the Achilles and the tortoise is referenced in Tolstoy's *War and Peace*.

Catch me if you can!

455 THE ARROW

ZENO'S first two paradoxes seem to rely on the idea that space is infinitely divisible. If it were not, then it would be entirely possible to begin your journey across the road, because there would be some distance that you would be able to traverse without first covering half of it. Unfortunately, Zeno anticipated this objection, and designed his paradox of the arrow to show that even if space is finite and discrete, motion is still impossible.

Consider the path of an arrow in flight. If space is discrete, then at each moment of its flight, the arrow must occupy some specific location in space. (This is just what it means to say that space is discrete.) However, if the arrow is occupying some specific location in space, then it is not in motion. The arrow cannot be in motion within a location, because there is nowhere to which it could move (each discrete location is indivisible). This means that at every point during its flight the arrow is at rest. Yet we know that arrows do in fact move (and that people cross roads and tortoises get beaten in races).

456 FAST FACT...

SENECA the Younger said: *"If I accede to Parmenides there is nothing left but the One; if I accede to Zeno, not even the One is left."*

457 FAST FACT...

SOME MATHEMATICIANS have claimed that Zeno's paradoxes can now be solved using modern calculus. However, philosophers maintain that this misses the central point of the paradoxes.

458 LIAR'S PARADOX

🎓 **EPIMENIDES**, a sixth-century BC philosopher from Crete, reportedly invented the Liar's paradox when he claimed that *"All Cretans are liars."* Somewhat ironically, this is not a strict paradox, but rather a statement that must be false (since if it were true, it would falsify itself). However, there is a more modern version of the puzzle that does seem to have genuinely paradoxical implications. Consider the following sentence:

THIS STATEMENT IS NOT TRUE.

This is known as the Strengthened Liar's paradox. If the sentence is false, then it must be true (because the negation of the claim that something is not true is that it is true). But if it is true, then it must be false (because the truth claim is precisely that it is false).

The usual way out of this paradox is to argue that self-referential statements of this nature are not properly meaningful. If this is right, then the sentence has no propositional content, which means the paradox disappears, because there is no claim here that could be either true or false.

459 FAST FACT...

📖 *"A man says that he is lying. Is what he says true or false?"* – the earliest known version of the liar's paradox, attributed to Eubulides of Miletus (4th century BC).

460 BURIDAN'S ASS

THE PUZZLE of Buridan's Ass is designed to satirize the idea that we don't have free will. It asks us to imagine that a starving donkey is standing precisely between two identical bales of hay. The donkey has been programmed to follow strict deterministic rules in choosing from which bale of hay to eat. The trouble is there is nothing in the donkey's past, nor in the situation in front of him, that enables the algorithm governing his behavior to select between the two bales of hay. It follows, then, that the donkey will stand in front of the hay trapped in indecision until he starves to death.

This is supposed to demonstrate that causal determinism is false, because it is unimaginable that no decision would be made in this sort of situation. However, a determinist can simply bite the bullet here, as Baruch Spinoza did, and allow that in a precisely balanced situation such as this one, indecision would indeed be the consequence.

461 FAST FACT...

THE BURIDAN'S Ass paradox is first found in Aristotle's De Caelo, which refers to a man who is as hungry as he is thirsty, and positioned halfway between food and drink.

462 FAST FACT...

JEAN BURIDAN was a medieval French priest. He never wrote about the "ass" paradox, but did put forward a theory of moral determinism, which the paradox satirizes.

463 SORITES PARADOX

🎓 **THE SORITES PARADOX**, attributed to the logician Eubulides of Miletus, comes in a number of different forms. Here is one version:

- *A man with 10,000 hairs on his head is not bald.*

- *If a man with 10,000 hairs on his head is not bald, then neither is a man with 9,999 hairs on his head.*

- *If a man with 9,999 hairs on his head is not bald, then neither is a man with 9,998 hairs on his head.*

  ...

- *If a man with 1 hair on his head is not bald, then neither is a man with no hair at all.*

- *Therefore, a man with no hair at all is not bald.*

The logic here seems sound. In essence, the claim being made is that subtracting one hair from any number of hairs can never make the difference between somebody being not bald and bald. This contention is entirely plausible, since "bald" seems to be a vague concept that does not allow such a sharp boundary. However, the difficulty is that this premise entails a conclusion that is obviously false – clearly a man with no hair is bald!

---

464 FAST FACT...

📖 **ANOTHER RESOLUTION** to the Sorites paradox is to appeal to group consensus as to what constitutes a heap.

465 FAST FACT...

📖 **TIMOTHY WILLIAMSON** and Roy Sorensen try to resolve the Sorites paradox by saying that there are fixed boundaries (beyond which something is no longer a heap), but these are necessarily unknowable.

466 PARADOX OF THE COURT

🎓 **PROTAGORAS,** the greatest of the Ancient Greek sophists, has agreed to teach oratory (public speaking) to the wealthy Euathlus on the following terms. Euathlus will pay half his tuition fees up front, and the remaining half on the day he wins his first court case.

The lessons proceed as planned, and Euathlus becomes a highly proficient orator. However, he does not take on a court case, and it becomes clear he never intends to, so Protagoras comes up with a wily scheme to get the money he is owed. He decides to sue Euathlus in court. He does not expect to win the case, but reasons that if he loses, then it means Euathlus has won his first case, so he will be obliged to pay the monies owed. On the other hand, if he does happen to win, it means the court has determined that Euathlus has to make good his debt. So either way Protagoras gets his money.

467 FAST FACT...

📖 **IN ANCIENT GREECE,**
Athenians had to represent themselves in court rather than hire lawyers, so it was essential that they learned to speak well.

Euathlus, of course, does not see it this way. He reasons that if he is victorious, then it means the court has determined that he does not have to pay the money; and if he loses the case, then he still has not won his first court case, so he is not obliged to pay the balance of the fees.

Who is right, and why? It is completely impossible to tell.

468 FAST FACT...

📖 **PROTAGORAS** was probably the first Greek to earn money in further education. He was notorious for his extortionately high fees.

469 THESEUS'S SHIP

🎓 **THE PUZZLE OF THE SHIP OF THESEUS** was originally formulated by Plutarch, a Greek historian and biographer of the first century BC.

> *"The ship wherein Theseus and the youth of Athens returned had thirty oars, and was preserved by the Athenians...they took away the old planks as they decayed, putting new and stronger timber in their place, insomuch that this ship became a standing example among the philosophers, for the logical question of things that grow; one side holding that the ship remained the same, and the other contending that it was not the same."*

The puzzle here is about identity, and specifically about what it means to say that some object in the present is identical with some object in the past. In this case, what is odd is that although the ship has entirely new constituent elements, we are inclined to say that it remains the same ship.

470 FAST FACT...

📖 **A SOLUTION** to the Theseus's ship paradox is to picture an object as a 4-D entity extending across time. The object is the same through all time slices, but individual time slices can differ from one other.

Although the issues involved here are complex, it seems likely that we are inclined towards this view because of thoughts about the spatio-temporal continuity of the ship

471 THE PLANK OF CARNEADES

CONTINUING WITH THE NAUTICAL THEME, consider the following scenario, which comes from the Ancient Greek philosopher, Carneades.

Two sailors are shipwrecked, and find themselves in the ocean, miles from anywhere, swimming for their lives. Happily, they spot a plank of wood, and both swim towards it. Unhappily, the plank will only support one of them. Sailor A arrives at the plank first, and clambers onto it. This means that Sailor B is destined to drown. However, rather than stoically accepting his fate, he shoves Sailor A off the plank, and paddles away at breakneck speed. As a consequence, it is Sailor A that drowns. Eventually, Sailor B is rescued, and confesses all to the authorities.

If a murder trial takes place, given that Sailor B would definitely have drowned had he not pushed Sailor A off the plank, can he claim he acted in self defence?

One interesting thing about this question is that there is a legal precedent for it in English law. R v. Dudley and Stephens (1884) found that it would not be permissible to kill another person in this sort of situation in order to save your own life.

472 THE PARADOX OF OMNIPOTENCE

🎓 **THE PARADOX** of omnipotence comes in a number of different varieties, but they all rely on the fact that it is possible to conceive of states of affair that an omnipotent being (i.e., God) would be unable to bring about. Here are a few examples:

- Can God create a rock so heavy that he would not be able to lift it?

- Can God create a lock that he cannot unlock?

- Can God create a mountain that he cannot climb?

Although these sorts of questions have a certain entertainment value, the puzzle they pose is not particularly difficult to avoid. The way out of it is to claim that omnipotence does not require the ability to do absolutely anything, it merely requires the ability to do anything that is logically possible. God cannot create square circles, or married bachelors, or rocks he cannot lift, but this is no impediment to his omnipotence as these sorts of things are not logically possible.

473 THE SURPRISE EXAM

YOU ARE HAPPILY SITTING AT HOME reading a philosophy book when suddenly a voice rings out from on high and announces that you will be examined on the book's content on a weekday next week, and that the exam will come as a surprise.

At first you are slightly annoyed but after you have thought about it for a while, you realize that the exam cannot take place.

The voice stated the exam would occur on a weekday next week, and that it will come as a surprise. Clearly, it cannot happen on the Friday, because if it has not happened by midnight on Thursday, then you'll know it has to happen on Friday, so it will not be a surprise. But this also means it cannot happen on Thursday, because if it has not happened by midnight on Wednesday, you'll know that it has to happen on Thursday (because it cannot happen on Friday), which again means it will not be a surprise. And then you realize this reasoning works for all the days backwards through the week, which leads you to conclude that the exam cannot take place at all.

However, this conclusion seems a highly counterintuitive. Not least, the fact you are now convinced the exam will not take place means you will actually be surprised whenever it does!

474 NEWCOMB'S PARADOX

YOU ARE ABOUT TO PLAY A GAME in which you stand to win a large amount of money. The rules are as follows. You will be shown two opaque boxes. Box A will contain $1000; and Box B will contain either $1,000,000 or nothing. You will then be asked to choose between taking home both boxes or just Box B.

The amount of money in Box B will be determined by a clairvoyant, whose predictions are 100% accurate, on the following basis. If he predicts you will take home both boxes, then no money will be placed in Box B. If he predicts you will only take home Box B, then $1,000,000 will be placed in Box B.

The prediction will already have been made, and the amount of money in Box B already fixed, by the time the game starts.

Should you take home both boxes or just Box B?

Robert Nozick said of this puzzle that everybody thinks it is obvious what should be done, but half think one thing, and the other half another, and both groups tend to think the other group is crazy.

475 FAST FACT...

ANOTHER version of Newcomb's paradox is the "idle argument": an all-knowing predictor has predicted the grade I will get in tomorrow's exam. Even if I don't know what the grade is, I can't change it, so what is the point of revising?

476 GETTIER'S COUNTER EXAMPLE

🎓 **AS WE NOTED** in a previous chapter, the "justified true belief" account of knowledge holds that somebody knows a fact, if (1) they believe it, (2) it is true, and (3) the belief is rationally justified. The counterexamples developed by Edmund Gettier are designed to challenge this account.

Imagine that Smith applies for a job, but has the justified belief that Jones will get the job. He also has the justified belief that Jones has 10 coins in his pocket. It follows, then, that Smith has the justified belief that the person who will get the job will have 10 coins in his pocket.

As it happens, Smith gets the job, and though he did not realize it, he also has 10 coins in his pocket. This means that Smith had a justified true belief that the person who got the job would have 10 coins in his pocket. But it is extremely implausible to suppose that he knew this to be the case, because he did not believe that he would get the job and had no knowledge of the coins in his pocket. It seems, therefore, that he had a justified true belief, but this did not equate to knowledge – he just got lucky.

477 FAST FACT...

📖 **EDMUND GETTIER** only wrote his famous 1963 paper challenging "justified true belief" at the urging of his colleagues, because he was short on publications. He has not published anything since.

478 FAST FACT...

📖 **GETTIER** was so unenthused by the three-page paper, he had it translated into Spanish and published it in an obscure South American journal.

479 FAST FACT...

📖 **ALTHOUGH** he was not interested in it himself, Gettier's paper has inspired many philosophers who still have not reached a consensus on an answer to his challenge.

480 A FRANKFURT CASE

IT IS OFTEN assumed that a person can only be morally responsible for what they have done if they could have done otherwise. The philosopher Harry Frankfurt developed a number of examples (now known as Frankfurt Cases) in order to challenge this assumption.

John has decided to kill Abraham. Mary thoroughly approves of John's decision, but she is worried he might change his mind. Consequently, she plants a chip in his head that can both read and implant thoughts. She decides to monitor John's thoughts, and then if he deviates from his intention to kill Abraham, she will activate the chip, ensuring that he goes ahead with his plan. If he does not deviate from his intention, then she will let him kill Abraham of his own accord.

As it happens, John does not have any second thoughts, the chip is not activated, and he kills Abraham of his own volition.

When presented with this scenario, most people say that John is morally responsible for killing Abraham. Yet it is also true that he could not have done otherwise. According to Frankfurt, this shows that people can still be morally responsible for their actions even if they could not behave in any way other than they do behave.

481 FAST FACT...

📖 **HARRY FRANKFURT'S** 1986 paper "On Bullshit" was republished as a book in 2005 and became a surprise bestseller, leading to media appearances.

482 FAST FACT...

📖 **HARRY FRANKFURT'S** later work focuses on the importance of love and caring.

483 DEREK PARFIT'S TELETRANSPORTER

🎓 **YOU STEP INTO A TELETRANSPORTER**, press the button, but nothing happens. You hear the clanking of the scanner as it records the location of every atom in your body, but you do not travel anywhere.

You step out of the teletransporter, and you are informed that it has malfunctioned. The correct information about your body was passed on to the replicator on Mars, and an exact copy of your body, identical in every detail, has been recreated. However, your original body here on Earth has not been destroyed, as it should have been, which is why it seems to you as if you have not gone anywhere. You are then given what you take to be bad news. You have been exposed to a fatal dose of radiation, and you are not going to survive more than a couple of days.

The question is, should you be consoled by the thought that your replica lives on? Your replica thinks that it is you. If the teletransporter had not malfunctioned, then your body on Earth would have been destroyed anyway. The only thing that is different here is that it is going to take a couple of days longer than you expected for the original version of you to cease to exist.

484 FAST FACT...

📖 **PHILOSOPHERS** such as Derek Parfit have made use of teleportation devices that have long been a staple of stories, from Aladdin to Star Trek.

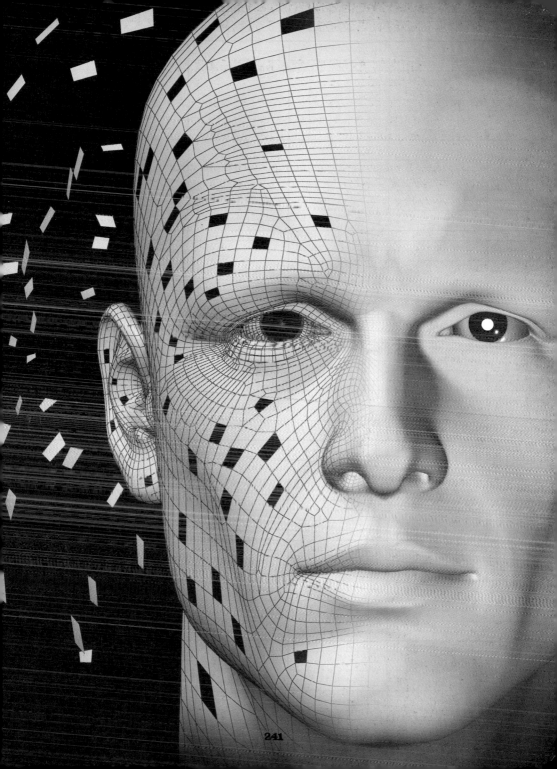

485 THE GRANDFATHER PARADOX

🎓 **IF YOU ARE A FAN OF SCIENCE FICTION**, then you are probably already familiar with the grandfather paradox. It asks us to imagine a person travelling back in time and killing their own biological grandfather before he has a chance to meet the person who would otherwise have become the time traveller's grandmother. This would make the time traveller's birth impossible (because one of his parents would never have existed).

However, if the time traveller had never been born, then clearly he could not have travelled back in time to kill his grandfather. This implies that his grandfather would have lived his original life, which in turn means that the time traveller would have been born, and would have been able to travel back in time to kill his own grandfather. So we have what appears to be a paradox.

486 FAST FACT...

📖 **THE GRANDFATHER PARADOX** was first described by science fiction writer René Barjavel in his 1943 book Le Voyageur Imprudent (Future Times Three).

There is no general agreement about what this thought experiment shows. Some people argue it suggests that time travel is impossible. Others claim that the problem is with the scenario itself, in that it cannot actually get started, because the very existence of the time traveller shows that even if he were able to travel back in time, he is destined never to kill his grandfather.

487 FAST FACT...

📖 **THE GRANDFATHER PARADOX** has been used to argue that backwards time travel must be impossible, or that the time traveller creates an alternative timeline in which he or she was never born.

488 FAST FACT...

📖 **IF A TIME TRAVELLER** is unable to interfere with history, it suggest a deterministic universe with no possibility of free will.

489 PARADOX OF DETERRENCE

👨‍🎓 **IMAGINE THAT YOU ARE THE RULER** of a country and that your nation relies on a nuclear deterrent for its security. This is necessary because your enemies have vastly superior conventional power. If your deterrent does not do its job, you know your homeland cannot win any war. It's true that in the event of an attack you could deploy your nuclear arsenal, but this will just bring untold death and destruction to the population centers of your foe's cities. It will not help you to repel the attack.

This means that if a hostile power launches an attack against you, there is absolutely nothing to be gained from carrying out the retaliation that constitutes the deterrent. However, if you know there is no good reason to retaliate once an attack occurs, then you cannot form the genuine intention to respond that makes the deterrent effective in the first place.

This sort of argument has led some people to countenance the possibility of a *"Doomsday machine"* that is programmed to retaliate automatically in the event of an enemy attack.

490 FAST FACT...

📖 **BRANDON CARTER,** author of the *Doomsday Argument*, is an Australian theoretical physicist best known for his work on the properties of black holes.

491 PARADOX OF JURISDICTION

ALBIE MALONE, a notorious racketeer, was shot and wounded by his rival, Barry Bowen, in Detroit in the fall of 1928. He was rushed to hospital in Chicago, where he lingered on the brink of death until he finally died of his wounds in the spring of 1929. In between times, Barry Bowen also met his death, in a hail of police bullets during a shoot out that occurred a few weeks after he shot Malone.

The puzzle about all this is that it is not clear who killed Albie Malone, or when or where he was killed. He cannot have been killed in the fall, when he was originally shot, because he was still alive in the fall. He cannot have been killed in the spring, because the person who shot him was dead by then, and dead people cannot kill.

It also follows that if he was not killed in the fall, then he cannot have been killed in Detroit, because his trip there in the fall was the only time he had ever visited Detroit. But equally he cannot have been killed in Chicago, because Barry Bowen, the man who shot him, had never visited Chicago, and was dead anyway by the time Bowen died.

So the question is, who killed Albie Malone, and when and where?

492 LONDRES EST JOLIE

🎓 **PIERRE LIVES IN FRANCE** and speaks only French. He has seen many pictures of a city called "Londres," and he has always been struck by how pretty it looks, so he is happy to tell people that "Londres est jolie."

One day, Pierre moves abroad to a town he knows only as "London," completely unaware that it is the same town as the one he calls "Londres." Unfortunately, he lives in a rough area, so he comes to think of London as being rather ugly. If he is asked about it, he will tell people, using the English he has picked up since he arrived, that "London is not pretty."

Therefore, it seems that Pierre believes both that London is pretty ("Londres est jolie") and that London is not pretty. Normally, if somebody assented to both these propositions, they would just be making a logical error. However, according to Saul Kripke, to whom we owe this scenario, in this case, it is not clear that Pierre is logically inconsistent in holding both these beliefs. After all, the problem here is just that he is not aware that "Londres" and "London" are the same place.

493 FAST FACT...

📖 **IN 2001,** Kripke was awarded the Schock Prize, philosophy's equivalent to the Nobel.

494 FAST FACT...

📖 **THE SCHOCK PRIZE** was first presented in 1993. Recipients receive around $60,000.

495 THE TROLLEY PROBLEM

🎓 **PHILIPPA FOOT** first specified the trolley problem as follows:

A trolley is running out of control down a track. In its path are five people who are tied to the track. Happily, it is possible to flip a switch, which will send the trolley down a different track to safety. Unfortunately, there is one person tied to that track who will be killed if you flip the switch. What should you do?

Most people say the right thing to do is to hit the switch, presumably because this will mean that fewer people will die. However, Judith Jarvis Thomson has come up with a variant of the problem that seems to suggest our moral intuitions are not entirely consistent here. The scenario is identical, except this time you are standing on a bridge under which the trolley will pass. A fat man is standing next to you, and the only way to save the five people is to push him off the bridge so that he lands in front of the trolley, thereby stopping it.

496 FAST FACT...

📖 **PHILIPPA FOOT'S** grandfather was President Cleveland.

The moral calculation seems to be the same here: one person sacrificed to save five. But this time most people think it would be wrong to push the man off the bridge.

497 FAST FACT...

📖 **DURING WORLD WAR II,** Foot shared an apartment with the novelist Iris Murdoch.

498 THE LOOP VARIANT

🎓 **THOMSON'S LOOP VARIATION** of the trolley problem is designed to challenge the notion that the reason it is wrong to throw the fat man off the bridge is because it would mean using him as the instrument to save the lives of the five people.

The loop variation is the standard trolley problem, with one added detail. This time the siding onto which the trolley has to be diverted to avoid running down the five people loops back onto the main track, which means the trolley will be sent back down the main track towards the five people, who will be run down anyway (in other words, the siding has the effect of turning the trolley around, and then sending it down the main track in the opposite direction).

As it happens, if the trolley hits the person on the siding, it will grind to a halt before it reaches the five people on its journey in the opposite direction down the main track. This means you can still save the lives of the five people, but only because you run down the single person on the siding. If he were not there, the five people would die anyway.

This situation seems analogous to the situation with the fat man on the bridge. The lives of the five people are only saved because the single person is there on the track. However, in this situation, most people will say it is morally permissible to turn the trolley.

499 FAST FACT...

📖 **A FURTHER** alternative to the trolley problem is that the fat man on the bridge is actually the villain who tied the people to the track in the first place. Would you push him off?

500 SIMULATION ARGUMENT

🎓 **THE SIMULATION ARGUMENT**, originally developed by Nick Bostrom, starts with the assumption that technologically mature civilizations will be able to create "ancestor simulations," which are "simulations of the simulators" predecessors – detailed enough for the simulated minds to be conscious and have the kinds of experiences we have."

The argument then asserts that one of the following propositions must be true.

- Almost all civilizations at our level of development become extinct before becoming technologically mature.

- The percentage of technologically mature civilizations that are interested in creating ancestor simulations is almost zero.

- You are almost certainly living in a computer simulation.

The most interesting possibility here is the last one. If the first proposition is false, then it means that most civilizations at our level of development eventually become advanced enough to create ancestor simulations. If the second proposition is also false, then it follows that a significant fraction of these civilizations will actually run these simulations. Therefore, if propositions one and two are both false, it means that there will be simulated minds just like ours.

501 FAST FACT...

📖 **ONE OF THE FIRST** references to simulations was by Philip K Dick in his 1959 novel *Time Out of Joint*, in which the main character is trapped in a bubble of 1950s small town America.

Bostrom argues that in this situation there will almost certainly be many more simulated minds than non-simulated minds, because there will be little cost in creating simulations. It follows, then, that if there are simulations, it is overwhelmingly likely that our minds are simulated, rather than real.

INDEX